Praise for Karen Noé and
We Consciousness

"*We Consciousness* shows us how to undo the optical
delusion of separation—which is the primary cause of all
lack and suffering—and thereby help the world evolve in the
direction of love. I recommend it wholeheartedly."

— **Robert Holden**, author of *Loveability* and
co-author with Louise Hay of *Life Loves You*

"Renowned psychic medium Karen Noé has the profound
ability to communicate with the deceased. In this awe-inspiring
book, *We Consciousness*, Karen discusses philosophical truths
that she has received from the late Wayne Dyer, ascended
masters, angels, and celestial beings. Filled with spiritual
insights, this book will reveal powerful principles that will
transform your life as you embark on this soulful path
to a more peaceful and joyous life."

— **Anita Moorjani**, *New York Times* best-selling author of
Dying to Be Me and *What If This Is Heaven*

"When we lost Dr. Wayne Dyer in August of 2015, I was sad for
myself for losing a friend and teacher, and also for the world for
losing such a powerful voice. I mourned the fact that we wouldn't
hear Dr. Dyer's wisdom and messages of hope at a time when we so
badly need them. Then I read Karen Noe's book, *We Consciousness*,
and I was comforted by reading the 33 messages of love and
compassion she shares. When I closed my eyes, I could hear Dr.
Dyer's voice as clearly as I did on his weekly radio show. I can rest
assured that we can still count on Dr. Dyer's wisdom as relayed
through Karen's gift of mediumship. Thank you, Karen, for sharing
with us these simple and powerful truths and reminding us that
our loved ones are just a thought away."

— **Diane Ray**, director of programming, Unity Media Network,
and former co-host with Dr. Wayne Dyer on his
weekly Hay House Radio show

"I had the great pleasure of meeting Karen Noé
several years back, and I instantly liked her. What struck
me about her was how incredibly humble and genuine
she is—despite the fact that her ability to communicate with
the world of spirit is up there with the best! In this new book,
We Consciousness, Karen takes this to an even higher level by not
only bringing through the messages of Wayne Dyer, but also
channeling the 33 most important truths that he, St. Francis,
and a litany of other wonderful guides and angels bring forth!
In my work with the Angel Margaret, she has often spoken of the
fact that we are all one and that we share the same consciousness;
the more we come to understand the truths of that connection,
the greater the chance we have to create heaven on Earth.
This book may well be the first step on that wonderful journey!"

— **Gerry Gavin**, author of *Messages from Margaret*
and *If You Could Talk to an Angel*

"As this beautiful book expertly illustrates, in order to
experience peace and love within, we have to express it without.
Love is the essence of the soul. This is part of the reason why I
felt so instantly drawn to Karen Noé. Karen doesn't just talk
about the importance of being an instrument of peace in this
world; she *is* that peace. She doesn't just talk about the importance
of giving and expressing love for others; she *is* that love.
True, Karen is a gifted psychic medium, but more importantly,
she is a caring, kind, loving person who truly wants to help others.
She is a blessing beyond words to me and so many. As you read
We Consciousness and the 33 profound truths brought through by
the late Wayne Dyer and others in the celestial realm,
prepare to be inspired and transformed."

— **Josie Varga**, author of *Visits from Heaven*, *Divine Visits*, and
*A Call from Heaven: Personal Accounts of Deathbed Visits,
Angelic Visions, and Crossings to the Other Side*

"Karen Noé, the internationally celebrated psychic medium and author, has penned a spiritual masterpiece with her new book, *We Consciousness*, which behooves all humans to embrace love, compassion, and forgiveness for all humans, Mother Earth, and all the creatures who share our planet. Ms. Noé, who channels wisdom from Dr. Wayne Dyer, St. Francis of Assisi, ascended masters, and other wise spirits, provides the reader with 33 profound truths that will open the door to the peace, harmony, and happiness we all yearn for our planet. She makes it clear that it is incumbent on us all to follow these truths to expand our consciousness, raise our vibrations, and become beacons of light for others to follow. This book is a must-read for those who want to transform our planet into a warm and loving home for all its inhabitants."

— **Garnet Schulhauser**, best-selling author of *Dancing on a Stamp, Dancing Forever with Spirit, Dance of Heavenly Bliss,* and *Dance of Eternal Rapture*

"We met Karen in person at a time of tremendous grief. Our husband and father, Dr. Wayne Dyer, had just recently crossed over, and we were feeling the enormous weight of that loss. Karen came into our lives, and from that moment on, each of us knew that our father was still with us. She has been an angel to all of us during these first few months of losing our dad, and her presence in our lives has been a gift we feel our dad orchestrated from the other side.

"Karen has the gift of talking to the angels and to loved ones who have passed, and her messages from our dad are so specific that we knew they could only be coming from him. Karen has given us the greatest gift during the first year of processing our loss; she has given us the knowing that someone who loves you never, ever leaves you. The comfort we have received from our time and conversations with Karen is indescribable. At times, it felt as though we were actually sitting there talking to our father and husband. We, as a family, have come to know Karen and to love her."

— **The Dyer Family**

"Karen Noé has a profound gift that she shares with the world, and this new book is more of her allowing us to witness her own desire to serve others. She is a blessing."

— **Marcelene Dyer**, Wayne's wife

"Karen Noé has proven to be a complete godsend to our family. . . . The timing and intensity of the messages are truly a gift from God, and I am forever grateful to have Karen Noé and her amazing gifts in my life."

— **Tracy Dyer**, Wayne's daughter

"Karen Noé is such a gift, and she has helped countless people learn how to heal and understand what happens after someone leaves us. I am forever grateful to her."

— **Skye Dyer**, Wayne's daughter

"Karen Noé is the real deal. Her gift has singularly changed my perception of life after death. . . . Karen has opened my heart and given me the gift of knowing that our loved ones are still with us, even after they die. For that I will be forever grateful."

— **Sommer Wayne Dyer Camp**, Wayne's daughter

"Karen's ability to communicate on behalf of my dad is truly astounding. I am so grateful that my dad placed her in our lives. She is a blessing to the entire Dyer family."

— **Serena Dyer**, Wayne's daughter

"This message from my father, through Karen Noé, allowed me to stay confident in the direction of my dreams, and brought me deep peace just at the moment when I needed it the most."

— **Sands Dyer**, Wayne's son

"Karen Noé has been an immeasurable guide in helping me learn to hear and feel my dad from the other side. She has given my family and me messages from my dad that are intensely personal and precise. I know without a doubt that Karen is communicating with my dad."

— **Saje Dyer**, Wayne's daughter

WE

CONSCIOUSNESS

ALSO BY KAREN NOÉ

*Through the Eyes of Another: A Medium's
Guide to Creating Heaven on Earth
by Encountering Your Life Review Now*

*Your Life After Their Death:
A Medium's Guide to Healing After a Loss*

All of the above are available at your local bookstore,
or may be ordered by visiting:

Hay House USA: www.hayhouse.com®
Hay House Australia: www.hayhouse.com.au
Hay House UK: www.hayhouse.co.uk
Hay House India: www.hayhouse.co.in

WE CONSCIOUSNESS

33
PROFOUND
TRUTHS
FOR INNER
AND
OUTER PEACE

KAREN NOÉ

HAY HOUSE, INC.
Carlsbad, California • New York City
London • Sydney • New Delhi

Published in the United States by: Hay House, Inc.: www.hayhouse. com® • **Published in Australia by:** HayHouse Australia Pty. Ltd.: www. hayhouse.com.au • **Published in the United Kingdom by:** Hay House UK, Ltd.: www.hayhouse.co.uk • **Published in India by:** Hay House Publishers India: www.hayhouse.co.in

Cover design: Angela Moody • *Interior design:* Nick C. Welch

Cataloging-in-Publication Data
is on file with the Library of Congress

ISBN: 978-1-4019-5231-0

1st edition, March 2018

Printed in the United States of America

To Annabelle, Emily, and Miles,
my rays of sunshine.
May you always have great dreams and
the faith to make them happen.
I love you so much!

CONTENTS

INTRODUCTION

I'm so honored to be a spokesperson for this very important topic. A number of significant events throughout my life have led me to write this book. Let me introduce myself. My name is Karen Noé, and I'm a psychic medium. People frequently ask me if I've always been able to connect with the celestial realm, and my answer remains the same: "I've always been psychic, but not always a psychic medium."

When I was a child, my psychic abilities manifested in multiple ways. I dreamed about things before they occurred, felt others' emotions as if they were my own, picked the "winning numbers" for my family, and so much more. I thought everyone was able to do these things with such ease, but in my later years I realized that this wasn't always the case. (However, people *can* learn how to tap into their psychic powers!)

I was extremely close to God through my younger years and was very religious, looking outside of myself for the answers. Now I consider myself more spiritual, and find all the answers within. Back then, I believed in God from what others told me about him; now I *know* God from what I have personally experienced.

When I was a child, comparing myself to other children, I realized I was different. I always felt compelled to get closer to God. I had read the Bible cover to cover many times, and I prayed the rosary every day. I would walk to the local church by myself often, and tried to attend Mass during the week, especially during Holy Week. I didn't tell anyone about what I was doing; I just did it. The more I felt my connection to God, the more I was aware of my connection to everyone else, and the more my psychic abilities continued to increase.

Then, about 20 years ago, when I was not feeling emotionally or physically well, I sat at the edge of my bed and asked God if I'd be okay. With that simple request, a huge glowing light began to come toward me from the other side of the bedroom. I was stunned and inwardly shouted, *If you are not of God, please leave!* Even after that request, the light continued to move toward me and eventually enveloped me with a sense of complete, unconditional love. All the negativity that had been within me dissolved in an instant, and I experienced an inner peace that words cannot even begin to describe.

Then I heard an audible voice say, *"Luce, lucina, bella luce lucina."* Since my grandparents were Italian, I knew what that meant—light, little light, beautiful little light. I began to weep and just *knew* that everything would be okay. (And it was!) Through meditation and dreams, I've since learned that the beautiful light was Saint Francis of Assisi. I had always felt a strong connection to him, and now I was able to feel and hear him speak directly to me.

Shortly after the experience with the light, I also began receiving profound messages from the angels. At first, the angelic messages were very strong. I then began receiving very significant messages from deceased loved ones as well. I eventually gave in and followed my intuitive guidance to relay these messages to others. These were what I call "without a doubt" messages, with evidence that only the deceased and their living loved ones would know.

The rest is history. Word spread, and I was eventually booked several months—then *years*—ahead of time. Primarily people have been coming to me to connect with their deceased loved ones. I've been doing this for a number of years now, and I love seeing how much my abilities have helped the living know that their deceased loved ones are truly with them.

The Importance of Raising My Energy to Connect to an Even Higher Realm

While I love giving and receiving messages from the other side, within the last few years, I have really missed connecting with the angels. I've also had many questions about life in general, but I wasn't receiving any answers. I finally realized the following very important concept: the answer to a question is never on the same vibration as the question itself. In order to feel and receive messages from those in the celestial realm, we must raise *our* vibration. When we are experiencing a negative emotion, such as fear, anger, despair, grief, or jealousy, our vibrational frequency is not on par with the energy of the angelic realm.

For example, several months ago, I couldn't stop thinking about a negative situation that arose around me. While I was still able to receive messages from those who had passed, I couldn't feel or receive any messages from the angels, and I became very frustrated.

I decided to go for a long walk with my dog. In my mind, I began to yell at the angels, *I know you can hear me—but I can't hear you! I need to hear from you again!* I kept repeating this over and over, but I didn't feel any response. I then had the urge to look up in the sky and saw a cloud shaped like a huge ear—with a finger inside of it. I didn't sense any meaning in it other than it being a very bizarre cloud formation.

Continuing to rant and rave in my mind, I yelled at the angels again, *I know you can hear me—but I can't hear you!* Frustrated, I picked up my pace and went home. As I arrived in front of my house a few minutes later, I suddenly noticed the gorgeous flowers in my yard. I could hear the beautiful melody of the birds singing in the trees. I went inside and felt so much love there. Feeling an abundance of appreciation for everything around me, I remembered the unusual cloud formation. Only *then* did I understand what it had meant.

The angels were telling me that they were always speaking to me—but I had my finger in my ear and wasn't listening to them! When I was angry and upset, I couldn't receive their beautiful messages, not even the amazing sign they had given me, because I wasn't on par with their energy. When I was grateful and saw the beauty all around me, I could feel my connection with the angels once again!

How May I Serve?

The yearning for more, however, continued. Still, I tried to remain focused on the peace and love all around me. I began to repeat to myself: *How may I serve? How may I serve?* I learned this phrase from Dr. Wayne Dyer, the internationally renowned author in the field of self-development and, in my eyes, the greatest inspirational speaker of all time. According to Wayne, if you ask the universe how you may serve, the universe will turn around and respond with, "How may I serve *you*?"

Because I always resonated with Wayne's teachings, I'd read most of his books and often listened to him speak. When my daughter was in college, she and I went together to see him in Boston, where he discussed *The Power of Intention*, his latest book at that time. After the event, my daughter wanted to stay so that Wayne could sign her book. Even though the line was extremely long, when it was our turn, he looked my daughter directly in the eyes and took the time to explain why it was important for her to always follow her dreams. These sincere and loving moments confirmed what I had known all along: this man stood for everything I believed and knew to be true. He cared and truly *was* an instrument of peace.

On August 30, 2015, my daughter called to tell me she had just learned that Wayne had passed away in his sleep. I couldn't believe it! I began to weep as if suffering the loss of my own best friend or family member. I couldn't eat dinner that night. I was so upset that the world had lost this amazing man who had literally changed the Earth for the better with his uplifting teachings!

Just a month later, I was scheduled to speak about life after death at Hay House's *I Can Do It* event in Orlando, Florida. I arrived a day early so that I could attend a tribute dedicated to Wayne. It was so beautiful, and yet very sad. His family members who were there seemed to be going through a difficult time. Although I'm sure they understood Wayne's spirit was still around them, they were still going to miss his powerful physical presence very much.

As I walked back to the hotel after this event, I spoke to Wayne inwardly. I requested that he be with me when I gave my speech a few days later, and asked him to give me a sign if he could really hear what I was saying to him.

I then inquired, *How may I serve?* Almost immediately after asking this question, an incredible peaceful feeling enveloped me. I heard Wayne's voice telling me that I was *already* serving.

Okay, I responded. *Then how may I serve . . . more?*

Signs and Messages from Wayne

When I arrived back at my room, I felt Wayne's presence so strongly. I became aware of an itchiness on my torso and reached down to discover a random sticker that had somehow attached to the inside of my shirt. It said "Disney World" in tiny letters on the bottom; however, I had not been there before this incident. My eyes grew large when I saw the real message: a huge *W* and small *e*. I then felt Wayne acknowledging that this was a sign from him, and I began to cry.

At first, I thought the *W*—*e* were the first and last letters of his first name, and I kept thanking him for giving me such an incredible "without a doubt" sign. However, after a series of life-changing encounters since then, I've learned that the letters on the sticker mean so much more. They were a symbol for the We Consciousness, which is the subject of this book!

Since his passing, Wayne has been coming through so many people around the world in dreams, thoughts, and miracles. He has been giving so many signs that it would take a book itself to contain them all. My favorite occurred during this same Orlando *I Can Do It* event. While looking out the window of my hotel room, I saw the most incredible rainbow directly over the conference center where the authors were speaking. I knew right away that it was

Wayne giving his family, friends, and fans another huge "without a doubt" sign, and I wondered which author was speaking at that time. I looked at the program and saw that it was Anita Moorjani, whom Wayne had loved dearly and had actively promoted. (Anita wrote of her miraculous near-death experience, shortly after which she was completely healed of her cancer, in her life-changing book *Dying to Be Me*.) Even though Wayne had left his physical body only a month prior to this incident, he had already been giving hundreds of these types of huge signs to people all over the world. It was truly incredible!

Later, through synchronistic events I'll discuss further on, four members of the Dyer family set up an appointment to see me in New Jersey. In the weeks prior to that appointment, every time I walked my dog, Wayne would come through with powerful messages. When his family members came to see me, Wayne was *so* excited to talk about the We Consciousness and what he was experiencing now, and he asked them if they wanted to hear about all of this or just personal messages. Of course they all said they wanted to hear the personal messages! I felt Wayne laugh because he wanted to share this profound information, but they wanted him to speak to each of them directly about "earthly" issues. Still, Wayne came through very strongly and spoke to each of them just the way he did when he was physically here.

Since then, Wayne's family and I have been texting, e-mailing, and speaking on the phone regularly. All the messages from Wayne are extremely specific and relevant to each of them. I am so humbled by this whole experience and delighted that I am able to hear what he is saying so clearly. Never in my wildest dreams had I ever imagined I'd be one of the messengers for this amazing man!

Why Did Wayne Choose Me as a Messenger?

I can feel and hear Wayne whenever he chooses or when I am in a state of positivity and love. It usually happens after meditation or after I summon those in the celestial realm and inquire, "How may I serve?"

Wayne revealed to me that I'm not his only messenger—there are many others, too! When I asked him why he chose me to be one of these messengers, he responded with, "Why did *you* choose *me*?" He explained that I am he, and he is me—but he is *everyone else* as well. This concept is, in fact, what the We Consciousness is all about. Although I didn't understand it at first, I was able to grasp everything much better as I received more messages from him and the We Guides about this truth. (In this book, I will share these same revelations with you!)

There are a few similarities between Wayne and me that I believe helped facilitate our connection. Like me, Wayne also had a very strong connection to Saint Francis of Assisi. I try to live by Saint Francis's words, "Make me an instrument of your peace." I know without a doubt that if more of us become messengers of peace, we'll be able to transform hatred, discord, and despair into love, harmony, and hope. We'll create heaven right here on Earth.

Additionally, as an empath, I'm usually able to see through the eyes of everyone I encounter throughout my day. When I do this, I am on the same vibrational frequency as Wayne because he is now able to perceive others in this way, too. (After we leave our physical bodies, we go through a life review where we are able to feel how we have affected every person we met as if we were the other person.)

Another reason I believe that I'm able to feel Wayne is the most obvious: I've had many years of experience in giving and receiving messages from those who have made their transition to the other side, so I'm able to hear him when he speaks to me. As a fellow Hay House author who was very familiar with his work, I was also in his frame of reference.

The Family Connection

Back in 2014, I'd interviewed Serena Dyer on my radio show, *The Angel Quest Radio Show*, as she was promoting her book, *Don't Die with Your Music Still in You: My Experience Growing Up with Spiritual Parents*. I really enjoyed this book and having her on my show. After her dad passed, I wanted to help Serena in any way I could, so I reached out to her. I sent her my book *Your Life After Their Death: A Medium's Guide to Healing After a Loss* to help her through the grieving process.

Shortly afterward, I spoke at the *I Can Do It* event in Orlando that I mentioned earlier. When Serena got on the bus going from the hotel to the conference center where the tribute for Wayne was being held, there was only one seat that wasn't occupied. That seat happened to be right next to me! Serena said that she had just received my book in the mail earlier that day and thanked me. As we chatted, I told her to look for signs from her dad because I knew he would be trying to contact her and the other members of her family. She told me that her youngest sister, Saje, already had an incredible dream in which she very clearly felt her dad. In the dream, Saje heard him speak and felt his arms hugging her. I told Serena that sounded like it was a true visitation!

About a week later, I received a message on Facebook from Saje, saying that Serena told her to get in touch with me so that she could ask me about the dream. Here's the wonderful dream, in Saje's words:

Last week, I slept a full eight hours for one of the first nights in a while. My alarm went off at 7 A.M., but I decided to hit snooze and sleep for another 10 minutes. As soon as I hit snooze, I was back in a dream state. However, in my dream, I was exactly where I'd been in reality—my bed in my apartment in New York City. Next thing I knew, I heard my door open, and Dad's voice as clear as day. In the funny sort of way he used to speak to me, he said, "Hey."

I immediately jumped out of bed and ran over to him, crying out, "Dad, are you really here?"

"Yes, I am really here!" he said.

Then I said to him, "Dad, I know I am asleep and dreaming, but this is not a dream; this is as real as anything that happens to me when I am awake."

He replied that this was real and that he was really there with me. I still felt a little skeptical, so I said to him, "Okay, if you are really here, then I can touch you."

He said in a funny, exasperated sort of way, "Touch me!" So I grabbed both his arms in my hands, and I could feel his hairy arms that were without a doubt his, exactly the way they were when he was alive. After that, I was convinced. I grabbed him, and we hugged each other.

I know we continued to talk, but I can't really remember what he said to me after that besides, "I love you, I am always here, and I will always love you." He also mentioned that I would continue to do his work, which is something he had been telling me for the last four or five years.

Then my dream started to take more of a typical dream essence. Somehow, he and I were sitting at a pool somewhere, putting our feet in the water, and my two brothers were there. And then I woke up.

I was *so* excited to explain to Saje how profound that dream was. There are several aspects of the dream that let me know it absolutely was a true visitation from her dad: It was a lucid dream in which she was aware she was dreaming. She had asked him what she needed to know, *and* he answered. Most important, she had also strongly felt the physical sensation of him hugging her.

I wrote to Saje to tell her it truly was her dad letting her know he was still with her! After messaging each other a few times and speaking on the phone, I offered to meet with her. She later asked if her mom and sisters Serena and Skye would be able to come as well. Of course I said yes. I was so honored and truly humbled to be of service to them.

As I was on my way to this appointment, a car with the license plate "DYER1" cut me off. (Excited, I took a picture to show Wayne's family, but it came out too blurry.) As I discussed earlier, Wayne came through loud and clear on that day with significant and specific messages for each of them. He continues to be larger than life in the celestial realm! (If you'd like to read the messages that his family members were willing to share, please visit Appendix B of this book.)

Connecting with the We Guides

Now here's the part I didn't expect. I thought I'd be channeling a whole book with messages just from Wayne. However, on New Year's Eve, as I was resting in the early evening, I entered an altered state of consciousness where I felt Wayne very strongly. He told me that now was the time for me to accomplish the goal that I had set for myself before I came here on Earth. I knew right away what that was: to spread the message of peace in the world!

Wayne told me that I wasn't going to channel just him, but others as well, including Saint Francis, ascended masters, and many angels—and together they would be presenting me with the 33 Profound Truths of the We Consciousness. He told me I've been channeling these other celestial beings for many years without knowing it, and I had all the information I needed within me. He told me it may be difficult for me to differentiate him and each individual angel and ascended master as they come through because they would all be uniting as one as they passed on their message. My mission would be to incorporate these truths into a book to promote peace on Earth.

Excited to begin this venture, I jumped out of bed and immediately started to put together the table of contents. This is the book you now hold in your hands. Thank you so much for coming with me on this journey.

I'll begin by sharing the 33 Concepts of the We Consciousness, and then I'll go on to explain how they all point to your becoming an instrument of peace. You will see that, after understanding and applying these ideas, you will be able to create heaven right here on Earth. My prayer is that these concepts will transform your life and the lives of all those around you.

≫ PART I ≪

THE
PROFOUND
TRUTHS
OF THE
WE
CONSCIOUSNESS

I asked Wayne if he'd like to include his own message at the beginning of this book, without the rest of the We Guides, and he came through with the following. It's important to note that I receive all messages as "downloads" of thoughts and feelings. Therefore, all the messages in this book are an interpretation of these downloads in my own words.

As you know, I'm still very able and happy to come through to my family, friends, and those who are asking for my guidance. I enjoy giving signs to all to show that I'm still here with them. However, at this time, I'm so excited to be on this journey that I've always anticipated with all those who had influenced me so much when I was there in a physical body—Jesus, Saint Francis of Assisi, Lao-tzu, and so many others. Joining forces with them is so much "bigger" than me coming through alone. I now see the tremendous significance of the We Consciousness. Whenever I was writing or speaking on stage, it never was just me—it was "We." When I was with my family and friends, it was me, and I was a different man!

Karen, I've come to you to give messages for my family and friends that only they and I would know so that everyone would realize I'm really still here with them. It's because of these messages that the world will see that it really is me, which is now part of the "We" coming through with the urgent message of spreading and being peace.

So yes, I'll still be coming through to you, but it'll be more than just me. I'll be stronger and larger because I'm coming through with the infinite possibilities of all there is! You've been connected to the We for many years on your spiritual journey of peace. Many times when you are with family and friends, you are still just "you."

By following the guidelines in this book, individuals will better be able to feel their connection with the Divine and all of creation, thereby becoming purer channels of peace.

So spread this important message now. I am with you!

CHAPTER 1

THE WE CONSCIOUSNESS

It does not matter what name you attach to it, but your consciousness must ascend to the point through which you view the universe with your God-centered nature. The feeling accompanying this experience is that of complete oneness with the Universal Whole. One merges into a euphoria of absolute unity with all life.

— PEACE PILGRIM

I am truly honored and humbled that I have been entrusted by Wayne Dyer and the We Guides to use my inner wisdom and knowledge to write the contents of this book by interpreting the 33 Concepts that they have given me. They were with me every step of the way, telling me when I needed to expand, add, or delete any of the information contained within these pages.

So, What Is the We Consciousness?

The We Consciousness is an awareness of the unity of everyone and everything, including animals and nature, our divinity, compassion for all of life, and what a person does to oneself or another affects the whole. If you can fully grasp these important truths, you'll be able to create miracles in your life and make a significant difference in the world.

The We Consciousness is broken down into 33 Concepts, which I have gone into detail describing below. (I also offer them in a simple list form in Appendix A of this book.) When I asked the We Guides why they chose the number 33, they revealed that 33 symbolizes Divine Guidance and the spiritual uplifting of all creation. Some of these concepts may seem to overlap others, but the We Guides assured me that they each have subtle differences.

The 33 Concepts of the We Consciousness

Concept I

The most important truth is that we are all one. Our oneness encompasses everything and everyone, including God, the angels, ascended masters, enlightened beings from other areas in the universe, deceased loved ones, animals, and nature.

This concept explains that you are not separate from anyone or anything else. While this is difficult to understand when you are here in the physical body, it can be realized through stillness and meditation. If your thoughts are going a mile a minute, you are ego-based and will not feel your connection to anything else. Therefore quiet time is imperative if you are serious about experiencing your connection to God, others, animals, nature, the angels, ascended masters, enlightened beings from other areas in the universe, and even your deceased loved ones.

Concept 2

Your becoming an instrument of peace is
vital to the survival of the planet.

Becoming an instrument of peace means to care for others and all of creation in a way that will literally transform and save the world. All you need to do is say to God, "Help me to become an instrument of your peace." You will then be shown ways to be of service to others.

Concept 3

The true essence of who you are is God. To say it in a different way, God is within every one of us—with no exceptions.

All of us are created from one Source; therefore this Source, or God, is within every one of us. When Wayne Dyer was in the physical body, he used the following analogy to describe this: If a person went to the ocean and scooped up some water in a cup, the water in the cup would still be the ocean water. Although the water in the cup wouldn't be the entire ocean, it would still contain all the elements of the ocean.

And so it is with us; while we are not the whole, we are part of the whole, with the same essence as that from which we came. In this way, God is within every one of us—with no exceptions!

Concept 4

*You are able to easily and effortlessly create
miracles in your life and in the lives of others.*

With God, all things are possible—and "all" leaves
out nothing that's of a loving nature! If you could realize
and reclaim who you really are (which is truly one with
God), you would understand that you are able to achieve
anything, including perfect health, abundance, love, sat-
isfying relationships, happiness, peace in your life and in
the lives of others, and so much more!

Concept 5

*God is only love and peace; you must be love
and peace to fully feel your connection with him.*

In order to feel your oneness with God, you must
focus on the love and peace within and around you. In so
doing, you will be raising your vibration to a higher level
and will be more on par with the energy of God and all
there is.

Concept 6

*You reinforce your connection to God
with positive thoughts and actions.*

When you think negative thoughts, you block your
connection with your Source of unconditional love.
Therefore it is important to make a conscious effort
to think more positively and act in a more loving and
peaceful way.

Concept 7

All animals are part of the We Consciousness.
To treat them with disrespect is to disrespect
yourself because they are one with you.

Animals are part of God's creation and are just as significant as humans. We must respect the rights and lives of *all* animals, not just our pets. To do otherwise is not only disrespecting them but also disrespecting ourselves as well, because they are part of us.

Concept 8

Our individual bodies create the
illusion of separation from the whole.

Because our souls are encased in separate bodies, we live as if we were disconnected from all others and fail to remember who we really are—one with God, the universe, and everyone else.

Concept 9

After you leave this world, you always feel
this connection to the whole because your body is
not separating you from everyone or everything else.

It will be easier to experience your connection to everyone and everything when you are free of your physical body. During this heavenly time, your unity will more clearly be revealed, since there will be nothing dividing you from the whole.

Concept 10

It is imperative to focus on what is right in the world,
instead of what is wrong.

If you wish to raise your vibration, instead of focusing
on all the problems in the world, direct your attention to
the abundance of beauty, love, and peace on our planet.
As James Redfield has perfectly stated, "Where attention
goes, energy flows."

Concept 11

At any particular time, the dominant vibration of the mass
consciousness strongly affects what is happening in the world.
Therefore it is imperative that more people become aware of
their connection to the whole and are at peace.

What the majority of the population is thinking and
feeling strongly affects the world. If more people would
be able to recognize that they are connected to the whole
and resonate with what is good within themselves and
others, the vibration of the planet would be raised, and
a more positive, peaceful energy would then dominate
the planet.

Concept 12

When most people are unable to feel their connection with
God and everyone else, world events occur that are not of a
peaceful nature. Since we are peace, we do not resonate with
these negative events when they happen. Yet the power of
light will defeat the power of darkness every time!

If most of the population feels negative and disconnected from the Divine, they will extend this energy outward, causing events that are not of a peaceful nature to happen. Since this is contrary to our true essence of love and peace, our higher selves will not be able to resonate with any of this, and it will feel wrong. Even with all this said, the vibration of the Divine will always be stronger and more powerful than any negative force. Therefore all we need to do is turn on our Divine light, and the power of the darkness will easily go away!

Concept 13

You are an infinite spiritual being having a temporary human experience on this planet.

It is important to remember that you are a spiritual being having a human experience, not the other way around. The physical body in which your soul is encased is finite and temporary, but the essence of who you are is limitless and eternal.

Concept 14

It is imperative to love and respect yourself, and understand that you are just as significant as everyone else.

It is just as vital to love and respect yourself as it is to love everyone else. God is within you, too, so when you do otherwise, you are disrespecting not only yourself but also the Source within you. Understand that you really do deserve all the good things that life has to offer you. You are worthy!

Concept 15

Once you leave your physical body, you are
able to perceive everything through God's eyes.

When you shed the shell that is encasing your real
self, you will be able to experience everything as God
does. You will finally see the bigger perspective and view
everything and everyone, including yourself, through the
loving eyes of Source.

Concept 16

After you make your transition, you are
able to see through the eyes of every living being.

When you leave your physical body, you will go
through a life review where you'll understand how you
have affected each person and animal, by seeing through
his or her eyes. You'll see how whatever you did or didn't
do unto others affected you as well.

Concept 17

We are all of equal power and love.
One is never more powerful than another.

Every one of us has God within, which means we are
all equal in the eyes of Source. When individuals believe
they are more powerful than others, it is an indication that
they are in the early stages of their spiritual development.

Concept 18

Forgive and ask for forgiveness.
When you forgive others, you forgive yourself.

Forgive those who have hurt you, and ask those whom you may have hurt to forgive you. When you hold on to anger, you are not only harming the other person but also hurting yourself. As the old saying goes, "Holding on to anger is like drinking poison and expecting the other person to die." Release the anger and you'll feel better, because in reality the other person is you!

Concept 19

You make the world a better place by
choosing to be an example of inner peace.

By maintaining peace within yourself, you'll create a more peaceful world. Your purer essence will be like a magnet, attracting peaceful individuals and situations all around you. This will generate the ripple effect of even more peace and tranquility that will spread all across the planet.

Concept 20

You are a co-creator with God and need
not be a victim of external circumstances.

Your true power is within, not outside yourself, and you have the capability of overcoming every obstacle in life. When you are fully able to grasp this concept, you'll understand the significance of shifting your emphasis from blaming others and feeling helpless to focusing on more positive, loving, and results-oriented outcomes.

Concept 21

How you feel about whatever you are observing creates circumstances in your life that will generate similar types of feelings within you. Therefore, in order to maintain inner peace, you must make a conscious effort to focus on the positive and disconnect from whatever is creating bad inner feelings.

The emotions that you are experiencing from whatever it is that you are observing will attract other situations in your life that produce these same types of feelings. Because of this, it is important to make a conscious effort to maintain strong, positive thoughts and disconnect from negative ones.

Concept 22

External objects or circumstances do not create inner peace.

Anything outside yourself will not bring you peace. There is a wise saying that states, "Peace comes from within. Do not seek it without."

Concept 23

You are not able to change others, but you are able to change your perception of them.

In order to maintain peace within, you must first realize that it is not your responsibility to transform others. Instead of focusing on what is wrong with them, choose to observe their love and light, and see through their eyes.

Concept 24

Healing occurs when the mind, body, and spirit are at peace.

In order for a complete healing to occur, the mind, body, and spirit must all be at peace. If any one of these elements is in discord, it will affect the other components in a negative way, and illness may occur.

Concept 25

Expect the best, just as God does.

When you anticipate the best will occur, you are behaving as God does. It is at this point that you will easily and effortlessly receive the finest outcomes in your life.

Concept 26

*In order to experience true inner peace,
you must live joyfully in the present moment.*

To experience peace in your life, it is imperative to choose to be happy right now, and not dwell in the past or worry about the future.

Concept 27

True faith can move mountains.

All things, without exception, are possible if you have full confidence about your desired outcome. As Jesus said, "Truly I tell you, if you have faith as small as a mustard seed, you can say to this mountain, 'Move from here to there,' and it will move. Nothing will be impossible for you."

Concept 28

*Problems cannot be solved with
the same energy that produced them.*

Problems begin with a negative way of thinking. The only way to fix a dilemma is to focus on a positive solution and experience the feeling of the situation being perfectly resolved.

Concept 29

*When you direct your attention to the love and light outside
of yourself, you expand the light within yourself as well.*

You increase your own vibration when you focus on the love and positivity all around you. This is why it feels so good when you direct your attention to the magnificence and perfection of all there is.

Concept 30

*Past, present, and future are all now.
Time is an illusion.*

After you leave your physical body, you will experience all blocks of time as if they were happening in the present moment. A great way to demonstrate this is with a ruler. Think of the six-inch mark and allow it to be the present time. All the numbers before it will symbolize the past, and all the numbers after it will symbolize the future. After your passing, instead of only being able to see the six-inch mark, you'll be able to see each of the inches and the entire ruler—all at once.

Concept 31

*Your true life's mission is
to spread the love that you are.*

Your main purpose here on Earth is to experience the love that you are and extend this love out unto others. It is not attaining the perfect job or climbing to a higher rank in society, although these positions may be a means through which you will be able to reach this goal on a grander scale.

Concept 32

It is in giving that you receive.

Since we are all one, whatever you give willingly and lovingly to others, you will receive back many times over. To say it another way, when you serve others, the universe will serve you as well.

Concept 33

These concepts are easier to understand when you remember who you are, from whence you came, and where you will go.

These concepts will make more sense to you when you fully realize

- your divinity,
- that you are interconnected with everyone and everything, and
- that your essence has existed before, and will continue to exist after you leave your physical body.

And so it is.

To conclude this chapter, I'd like to share this beautiful quote by Black Elk, which perfectly sums up the significance of these profound truths:

"The first peace, which is the most important, is that which comes within the souls of people when they realize their relationship, their oneness with the universe and all its power, and when they realize that at the center of the universe dwells the Great Spirit, and that this center is really everywhere, it is within each of us."

CHAPTER 2

BECOMING AN INSTRUMENT OF PEACE

*Imagine what 7 billion humans could accomplish
if we all loved and respected each other.*

— ANTHONY DOUGLAS WILLIAMS

Every concept of the We Consciousness points to our oneness with God and others or extending our true essence of peace onto all of creation. If we all could fully understand and live by these concepts, violence wouldn't even be considered an option, and we'd all be living in perfect harmony with each other. Or, to say it a different way, if we were all able to see the world from the perspective of the infinite peace we are, there would be nothing *but* peace in the world!

There are a few people in history who were fully able to do this, including Jesus; Saint Francis of Assisi; Martin Luther King, Jr.; Mother Teresa; and Nelson Mandela, among others. Each one of them, in his or her own way, was able to raise the vibration of the planet!

But what about you? Did you ever consider the possibility that *you* could be the one to create peace on Earth and change the world? I'm saying you absolutely can, but you first have to reclaim your power and remember who you really are.

The Essence of Who You Are

Again, you are one with everyone and everything. You are not separate from God or from others. Even though you may be only one person, your thought forms actually do affect others in a big way!

If you have negative thoughts, those around you who have similar or lower vibrations are constantly being reinforced by these thoughts. On the other hand, when you have positive thoughts, you influence everyone around you in a positive way. In other words, negative energy cannot penetrate into the higher levels of energy, but the higher levels of energy can penetrate into the lower levels. This is because positive energy has a higher and stronger vibration than negative energy, which has a slower and weaker vibration.

To take it a step further, because of our oneness with everything, harmful or negative ideas and activities in one part of the world really do affect those on the other side. If our thought waves are positive and loving, the vibration of love multiplies, creating harmony and kindness with others. On the other hand, if our thought waves are negative, they create anger, greed, violence, and other negative energy. These thought forms are drawn to similar thought waves all over the world and merge with them, creating the ripple effect of even more negative energy.

Even though we appear to be separate from everyone else, we are linked to each other's thoughts at all times. Your thoughts are energy, and energy is real. If your thought forms are of a loving nature, you can actually achieve peace, not only for yourself, but also for the entire world. It makes sense, then, to say that if you want peace on Earth, you must first remember to keep your own thoughts on peace and harmony.

Begin with Five Easy Steps

You may be wondering what you can do to set this life-changing journey of peace in motion. Here are five simple steps you can take to begin this process:

1. If there are so-called bad events taking place around you, visualize and *feel* the new, positive situations you want to create instead of "what is."

In so doing, you will begin the manifestation process of replacing these negative situations with more powerful, loving, and peaceful ones!

2. Pray for inner and outer peace.

When you pray, make sure to feel the peace as if it is already occurring in the present moment. Phrase it as a positive statement, like "Thank you, God, for expanding the peace within me and allowing peace to prevail on Earth." *Know* as you pray that whatever is needed to obtain this peace is happening right now.

3. Quiet your thoughts.

By meditating daily, you'll actually be able to *feel* your connection with God and everyone and everything.

4. Call upon the angels to help you the next time someone's negativity disrupts your peaceful mind.

Ask Archangel Michael to encircle the room you are in with as many angels as are needed to remove the negative energy that are you are experiencing. Then call upon the angels to surround the person who is infringing upon your space and send them peace, too. The only way to put a stop to the ripple effect of negative energy is to begin a new ripple effect of positive energy.

The other person will not consciously know what you have done, but subconsciously he will. He will feel the positive energy directed his way and will cease to feel the need to send negativity in your direction. Try it—it really works!

5. Send love to *everyone* in your path.

By extending love to all, you will be raising not only your own energy but also all the energy around you. Albert Einstein is reported to have once said, "Nothing happens until something moves." In other words, we need to do something to *change* our way of thinking and acting in order to become an instrument of peace. In this way, we can create the peace that is very much needed on Earth, or else hatred, war, and violence will continue to exist. Begin your new way of positive thinking today. Your life will be so much better from it, and so will the lives of everyone in your path.

Yes, you really *can* make a big difference in your world and the world around you. Focus on the positive and use your energy to expand upon what you want (which is peace), not on what you don't want (which is conflict). Because we are all one, begin by cooperating with others. Help as many people as you can during the day. Instead of just worrying about how events will affect just *you*, understand how your actions will also affect others. In so doing, you will become an instrument of the peace that God intended.

Similarities of the Prayer of Saint Francis and the Concepts of the We Consciousness

It is now very fitting for me to briefly speak about what I feel is one of the most beautiful peace prayers of all time: the Prayer of Saint Francis. Its main focus is on your becoming an instrument of peace and serving the world. You will see that there are so many similarities between this prayer and the concepts of the We Consciousness.

Prayer of Saint Francis

Lord, make me an instrument of your peace.
Where there is hatred, let me sow love;
Where there is injury, pardon;
Where there is doubt, faith;
Where there is despair, hope;
Where there is darkness, light;
Where there is sadness, joy.
O divine Master, grant that I may not so much seek
To be consoled as to console,
To be understood as to understand,
To be loved as to love;
For it is in giving that we receive;
It is in pardoning that we are pardoned;
It is in dying to self that we are born to eternal life.

This prayer focuses on extending our love and concern outward instead of demanding it only for ourselves. If we could fully understand that others *are* us, we'd be able to comprehend the meaning of the quote, "Whatever we do unto others, we do unto ourselves." When we extend our love, pardon, faith, hope, light, joy, and understanding to others, we truly receive them back as well!

However, I want to add a crucial point here. In order to extend these gifts to others, we must first feel peace within *ourselves*! We must *expect* to see peace everywhere, and also acknowledge the infinite peace that *we* are. Then we must live that identity to the fullest.

In the next part of this book, I'll explain *how* to obtain this inner peace by understanding that we are part of the We Consciousness and are just as significant as everyone else. In other words, we deserve the same love and respect that we give to others!

 *PART II*

SELF-LOVE

Before I began this section, I asked Wayne to come through with whatever he needed to say about self-love. Here are my words to describe the downloaded message he gave at that time.

Always remember to love yourself first. My dear friend Anita Moorjani is correct when she says, "Our feelings about ourselves are actually the most important barometer for determining the condition of our lives!" Love begins inside us.

The stars illuminate from within and shine their own light outward over the universe, just as you do. Nourish yourself first so that you'll be able to share your magnificence with the world. When you love yourself, you are loving everyone, because they all are *you! You have to turn your inner dimmer switch all the way up before you can enlighten the world.*

Let me just add here that being selfish and loving oneself are not the same. There were times when I was in the physical body that I had a healthy ego and made sure my needs were met. I'm now able to see my life from a grander perspective and understand how this sometimes affected others negatively, and I'm sorry for that. So I would tell everyone to try this: step back to see if loving yourself will help or hurt others.

Yes, you must nurture yourself before you'll be able to share this love with others. The key is balance; just make sure to see how you are affecting others as you love yourself. And, perhaps more important, take notice of how loving others is affecting you!

Think about that cell phone you keep recharging. When it runs out of power, the phone is of no use to you. You have to plug it in and charge it again, and you must do this frequently! So it is with you. You must make it a priority to recharge yourself daily. Only then will you be able to serve the world. As I always said when I was there in the physical, "You can't give to others what you don't have inside of you."

When you ask the universe, "How may I serve?" make sure to add the words "myself and others!" Always remember, it's all about balance!

I'll be there to guide you and anyone who needs my assistance with this.

Maintaining inner tranquility is the first and most significant step to creating peace on Earth. As Peace Pilgrim stated so perfectly, "When you find the peace within yourself, you become the kind of person who can live at peace with others."

This section of the book will be devoted to showing you how important it is to treat yourself as the magnificent, Divine being that you are. To restate Concept 14 of the We Consciousness: *It is imperative to love and respect yourself, and understand that you are just as significant as everyone else!*

CHAPTER 3

THE ILLUSION OF BEING SEPARATE FROM GOD AND OTHERS

*A sense of separation from God is the
only lack you really need correct.*

— A COURSE IN MIRACLES

Remember, it isn't possible to ever be disconnected from God, everyone, or everything. The link is always there; you just have to plug into this energy to *feel* it. It's essential to work on loving yourself so you are more on par with the energy of the infinite peace of who you really are. As Concept 5 states: *God is only love and peace; you must be love and peace to fully feel your connection with him.*

It's also imperative to see the perfection of everything and everyone around you. God is pure love, so to experience anything but love in a situation separates you from your true essence. Therefore, in order to be on par with the energy of the Divine, it's necessary to always focus on the positive. When you focus on the good around you, you also reinforce the magnificent light that is within you, and you will feel good! As Concept 6 states: *You reinforce your connection to God with positive thoughts and actions.* And as Concept 29 states: *When you direct your attention to love and light outside of yourself, you expand the light within yourself as well.*

Self-Love Begins with a Better Awareness of the We Consciousness

As perfectly stated by Wayne Dyer when he was still here in the physical, "Somewhere along the line, we have created the illusion that we are separate from God and others. We have created the illusion that we are what we have or what we do. We have created the illusion that we need to be better than others. We have also created the illusion that because we are separate from our Source, we do not have the power of the Source." This incorrect way of thinking has prevented us from experiencing the total love and peace that we truly are. When we're able to remember that we really are one with God, we'll understand that we are able to create *anything* of a peaceful nature in our lives!

However, we must first raise our vibration to be more on par with the energy of the Divine. (I will go into more detail on how to do this in Chapter 7.) We can also remind ourselves of our connection to the whole by repeating affirmations throughout the day. Affirmations are positive statements told from the first-person point of view *affirming* that all is well in your world. Louise Hay, motivational author and founder of Hay House, created many affirmations that I find wonderfully helpful. I've included several below. Try saying them to yourself throughout your day, and make up others to affirm what you want to see more of in your life.

- I am connected to all of life.

- Each person is part of the harmonious whole.

- I help create a world where it is safe for all of us to love each other.

- What is true of me is true of everyone. We are all learning to look within ourselves to find the wisdom to live harmoniously.

You Are Unique within the Oneness—and That Is Good!

One hand generally has five fingers on it, but none of the fingers are exactly alike, and each has a different job to do for the hand. So it is with each of us. Although we are all one, each of us carries certain truths and experiences within ourselves. We are all connected to God, but each of us has a different reason to be here. Therefore we must accomplish what we chose to do before we came to Earth, not what others want us to do. We need to go within ourselves and seek our own personal truth.

In order to experience peace within, it's imperative to question everything that comes into our awareness from outside ourselves, and see if it feels right to us. Even though we may say we *believe* certain ideas, if the information doesn't come from within ourselves, we may experience an element of doubt about these views. What is true for another person, or even the masses, may not be true for us. So it is very important not to go along with everybody just because it is the popular thing to do.

Looking back throughout history, you can see that those who have made significant differences in the world were those who dedicated their lives to living their dreams. They did whatever they needed to do to achieve their purpose, regardless of what others thought and despite any obstacles in their paths. Think of Jesus; Albert Einstein; Martin Luther King, Jr.; Mahatma Gandhi; Michelangelo . . . The list can go on and on. They changed the world in their own way by reclaiming the power within and devoting their lives to living *their* passion. In other words, they helped the masses by honoring their own special calling!

If you have not found your life's purpose, please don't despair. You are so loved, and you are here for a reason. The fact that you are here on Earth is evidence of this! The most important thing for you to do is really listen to your soul. As Steve Jobs said, "The only way to do great work is to love what you do. If you haven't found it yet, keep looking. Don't settle. As with all matters of the heart, you'll know when you find it."

You *know* what makes you come alive. You *know* what your passion is! Whenever you get excited about something, it's your soul telling you, "Pay attention; this is an important part of my soul's journey." Do not ignore this inner prompting. Remember to let the amazing light within you shine, and always be yourself. You came here for a magnificent purpose, and you should never suppress your uniqueness to fit in with others.

Others might not agree with what you should be doing with your life. Please do not allow these naysayers to take you away from your calling. On the other hand, make sure to allow others to be who they are; accept them, as long as they are not hurting anyone. If we accept them for who they are, they will be free to accomplish what they came here to do. Then they, too, will be at peace.

What We Do to Ourselves Affects the Whole

Because we are not separate from God and others, what we do to ourselves really does affect the whole. When we neglect ourselves, we're abandoning God and others. When we disrespect ourselves, we're disregarding the whole. When we focus on the darkness, we're not allowing the God within us to shine.

On the other hand, when we lovingly take care of ourselves, we're treating the whole with reverence. When we respect ourselves, we're honoring all that is. When we focus on the light, we're seeing the world as God does. When we heal ourselves, we're healing the world around us. When we cherish ourselves, we're in a better position to love others. When we devote more time to self-care, we feel refreshed and more willing to designate time to serving others.

My own personal experience lets me know how true this is, and one particular example comes to mind. For many years, my appointments for readings and healings have been booked out years in advance. In the early years of my career, I'd work seven days a week, never giving myself a day off. This depleted my energy so much that I had nothing left to give others. Then, somewhere along the line, I decided that I wasn't going to do weekend appointments anymore. Immediately after making that decision, I felt as if a weight had been lifted from my shoulders, and I experienced an incredible inner peace.

I'd been hesitant to make this change because I was worried that some clients wouldn't be able to see me anymore. In other words, I was putting their perceived needs ahead of my own. However, after I announced my new schedule, everyone was more than willing to work around it! Because it helped me feel refreshed and energized, I was able to give so much more of myself to everyone else. It was a win-win situation for everyone! However, I had to honor myself *first* so I could then serve others better.

Again, you are not separate from others, and what you do to yourself really does affect the whole. In other words, you must love and respect yourself before you can give love to others. However, it's just as important to love yourself because you are as significant as everyone else. Simply put, you *deserve* to feel better!

Are you the type of person who always puts everyone ahead of yourself? Please realize that when you sacrifice every bit of your time to others, you don't have quality energy left to offer. So think about what you can do for yourself that will actually benefit everyone else as well. Then do whatever you need to do to make that happen!

Take a break from working to clear your mind. Go to your favorite spot and pick up something you love for lunch. (You have to eat anyway!) Turn off your cell phone when you don't want to be interrupted. Say no to anything you don't want to do.

I'll be discussing even more things you can do to make yourself feel better in the next few chapters, but I'm sure you get the picture. Then I'll talk about the many amazing benefits you'll receive after you are finally able to recognize the magnificent light that you are!

CHAPTER 4

PATHWAYS
TO LOVING
YOURSELF

*You can search throughout the entire universe for someone
who is more deserving of your love and affection than you
are yourself, and that person is not to be found anywhere.
You yourself, as much as anybody in the entire universe,
deserve your love and affection.*

— ATTRIBUTED TO THE BUDDHA

Before you can *give* love and peace to the world, you
must first *have* love and peace. In order to *have* these
qualities, you must first *experience* them within yourself
and know that you *are* worthy of everything that life has
to offer!

You might be saying to yourself, *How will I ever be
able to experience these qualities within when all my life I've
put myself last?* Well, the answer is quite simple: to begin
this process, it's essential to *remember* who you really are!
According to the We Consciousness, you *are* love because

you are one with the Source of this magnificent love. With this newfound wisdom, you could never put yourself down again!

To get you started, here are 10 important pathways to self-love. Be gentle and patient with your progress, and allow your amazing light to shine through. As a wonderful by-product, when you permit the powerful love within you to expand, everyone around you will also be healed, just by being in your incredibly radiant presence!

10 Pathways to Self-Love

1. Be yourself and honor your truth over society's demands.

You are unique within the oneness—and that is *good*! Allow your beautiful light to shine, and evolve to attain all the goals you intended before you came here on Earth. You came into this world for a reason, and that reason doesn't involve blending in with everyone else just to be accepted. It's more important for *you* to accept you!

It is perfectly okay if others do not understand your journey. Don't let them change or mold you to become what they want of you. This brings to mind a wonderful quote from Dean Jackson: "When she transformed into a butterfly, the caterpillars spoke not of her beauty, but of her weirdness. They wanted her to change back into what she always had been. But she had wings."

So live your truth and honor your ultimate purpose in life. Spread *your* gorgeous wings and fly!

2. Reclaim your power.

You have the power of God within you! You must fully grasp this concept if you are going to reach your full potential. I *know* this isn't always easy. For most of my life, I've always put everyone first and thought others were better than myself. As a matter of fact, right before I began communicating with Wayne Dyer and the We Guides, I had a severe "feeling insignificant" attack.

During the aforementioned Hay House *I Can Do It* event in Orlando, I was sitting on a bus with my favorite authors and members of Wayne Dyer's family. Serena Dyer took a seat next to me, and although I felt very connected to her, I felt so insignificant. Afterward, I decided to walk back to the hotel instead of taking the bus, because I felt I didn't fit in. After all, I was not a member of the Dyer family and not as important as all those authors.

As I was walking to the hotel, I began asking, "How may I serve?" Then I heard Wayne Dyer's voice, telling me that I was *already* serving. An incredible peace overcame me, yet I still responded with, "But I am so insignificant!"

Get out of your own way! Wayne forcefully told me.

What? I asked myself. *Am I really hearing this?* I asked Wayne to give me a "without a doubt" sign so I'd know he was really with me. Within a matter of minutes, I received the wonderful sign I spoke of in the Introduction (the *We* sticker)!

The next day while at an author party, I was again feeling insignificant and like I didn't fit in, even though I too was a Hay House author. It continued to bother me, and I couldn't sleep that night, so I did some energy work on myself to feel better. Little did I know that this particular learning experience was going to change my whole life!

I performed an exercise by Donna Eden (the most sought-after spokesperson for energy medicine) called "Expelling the Venom." I stated over and over, "I am feeling insignificant," as I raised my arms in the air, then swung them down forcefully with a huge sigh as I attempted to blow out this negative feeling. After doing this exercise a number of times, I felt remarkably better! I was able to say with full conviction, "I *am* significant! I *am* significant!" (You can find out more about this technique by searching online for "Expelling the Venom" by Donna Eden, or picking up her book *Energy Medicine*.)

The next day, I felt so wonderful and empowered. I was amazed to have released unwanted thoughts and feelings of insignificance that I'd been carrying around for many years! I spoke at the *I Can Do It* event about life after death and how to heal after the loss of a loved one. At the end of my lecture, I even received a standing ovation.

I then felt Wayne say to me, *Yes, you are significant—and so is everyone else. You are making a difference, as can everyone in this room. Each of them has to reclaim their power, just as you did!* Shortly after this experience is when I began receiving this wonderful information about the We Consciousness.

In order for all this to happen, I needed to first release all of my insecurities about not being good enough. Only then was I able to achieve what I came here on Earth to do: promote peace and healing in the world.

And so it is with you. Reclaim your power and understand your significance in being here on Earth! No more shrinking and blending in with everyone else. You are special, and it's time to allow everyone to benefit from your magnificence. You have God within you—remember who you are! Marianne Williamson said it best: "Your playing small does not serve the world. There is nothing enlightened about shrinking so that other people will not feel insecure around you. We are all meant to shine as children do."

3. Do what you love *now*.

As Concept 26 of the We Consciousness states: *In order to experience true inner peace, you must live joyfully in the present moment.* So get excited about this day! What are you doing today that you really love doing? Don't wait until tomorrow or a more perfect time. Do whatever it takes to make you happy—right now. Surround yourself with people and situations that make you feel good. For example, if you are in a job that doesn't make you happy, feel what it would be like in this moment to have the perfect job, and then take the necessary steps to allow that to happen.

4. Meditate to experience peace within.

If your thoughts are going a mile a minute, you won't be able to feel your connection with God or the rest of the We Consciousness. Set aside time each day, even if it's only 10 minutes, to empty your thoughts so that you'll feel your connection to all there is. In this quiet time, you'll experience the amazing peace that you will never find anywhere else! As Concept 22 says: *External objects or circumstances do not create inner peace.* Go within to feel real inner joy!

5. Treat your body as the temple of God that it is.

Your body encases not only the very essence of who you are but also the God within you. In order to feel good, you must devote your attention to keeping it healthy. Eat nutritious meals, drink plenty of water, exercise, and get the rest that you need. Be mindful of honoring the precious vessel that houses your Divine spirit!

6. Forgive yourself.

There's no point in dwelling in the past. Realize you did the very best you could under the circumstances, with the knowledge that you had at the time. Blaming yourself will only keep you stuck in the same negative energy as whatever it was that you feel you did wrong.

You can learn from your mistakes and replace your negative actions with more positive ones. Go through each of the so-called damaging events in your mind, and replay them with whatever you should have done instead. Try to understand *why* you did what you did.

It's important to recognize that you're going to make some mistakes in life, and that's okay! Learn from them and forgive yourself because you didn't know any better at the time.

7. Focus on love and the many blessings around you.

There is *so* much beauty and tenderness in the world. Make it a common practice to notice all of these amazing, uplifting occurrences. As Concept 29 states: *When you direct your attention to the love and light outside of yourself, you expand the light within yourself as well.* Concept 10 says: *It is imperative to focus on what is right in the world, instead of what is wrong.* The world is a glorious place, so don't focus on the negative and miss out on the magnificence around you.

8. Respect yourself.

Practice self-love. Say no when you are asked to do something you do not wish to do. Stop all self-criticism. Stand up for yourself when needed. When you are kinder and gentler with yourself, others will value you more as well! Louise Hay said it perfectly: "Love yourself as much as you can, and all of life will mirror this love back to you."

9. Take note of your good qualities.

Spend time each day honoring all your positive attributes. Pay attention to general qualities, such as "I'm a kind person," "I have a lot of patience," and so forth. Also notice what you have done throughout the day that you are particularly proud of, such as "I helped my friend get through this difficult time," "I'm proud that I finished cleaning out my closet," and so on.

It helps to jot down these characteristics so you can revisit them at a different time. Writing yourself a letter of appreciation is a perfect way to do this. (I will show you how to write this type of letter in Chapter 8.)

10. Have fun!

Life is meant to be enjoyed. Smile often, laugh, and dance. Be childlike, silly, and spontaneous. Always take time throughout the day just to play!

Loving Yourself Creates a Ripple Effect of More Love

Your thoughts create your reality, whether you are aware of it or not. Concept 21 states: *How you feel about whatever you are observing creates circumstances in your life that will generate similar types of feelings within you. Therefore, in order to maintain inner peace, you must make a conscious effort to focus on the positive and disconnect from whatever is creating bad inner feelings.* This includes the emotions and thoughts you have about yourself. If you have negative inner thoughts about yourself, you'll attract pessimistic people and negative circumstances in your life. On the other hand, when your thoughts are focused on self-love, you'll attract loving situations and those who will treat you in a tender, caring way.

This love will create a ripple effect that extends outward to others as well. As Concept 19 states: *You make the world a better place by choosing to be an example of inner peace.* Practicing self-love guarantees a favorable outcome for everyone involved. So begin loving yourself right now, and you'll create a more peaceful place for yourself and for all those around you.

Remember, you are not being selfish by practicing self-care. Start the journey of creating peace on Earth by beginning with the most important person in your life—*you!* Love everything about yourself, with no judgment. Love the part of yourself that created every single person and situation in your life. (Yes, in reality, each person in your world is you, and every situation surrounding you was created by you!)

If you really want to become an instrument of peace, you first need to maintain a high regard for your own well-being and happiness. Start the process by contemplating what you'd like to hear from others. Do you want them to say that they love you, they appreciate you, you made a difference in their lives, or they forgive you? You will quickly see that whatever you most desire to hear from others is what you need to tell yourself! Look in the mirror and tell yourself how great you are. Appreciate yourself for who you are and the difference you are making in the world. Forgive yourself for anything you have done in the past, acknowledging that you did the best you could under the circumstances.

In the next chapter, I'll discuss the many benefits of loving yourself, so you'll see your efforts will not be in vain. Just be patient and I promise you, it will all be worth it. Now repeat after me: "I love you, [*your name*]. I really love you!"

CHAPTER 5

BENEFITS
OF
SELF-LOVE

Self-love is the source of all our other loves.

— PIERRE CORNEILLE

Loving yourself is the first essential step to creating peace in your life and in the lives around you. After practicing self-love on a regular basis, your whole life will change! You'll finally realize that you are entitled to the magnificent blessings the world has to offer; you'll be more fulfilled, more independent, and so much happier. It'll be a win-win situation for all, because everyone around you will benefit, too.

There are 12 amazing benefits you'll receive when you practice self-love. Begin right now on your wonderful new journey of recognizing the delightful, precious being that you truly are.

The 12 Main Advantages of Self-Love

1. You will make your own happiness a priority and not be swayed by external conditions.

When you begin to love yourself, you'll make sure you are happy right *now*, regardless of what is happening in the world. As Concept 26 says: *In order to experience true inner peace, you must live joyfully in the present moment.* You'll recognize your many blessings and not be influenced by negative people and events.

2. You will look out for your best interests.

You'll always "have your own back" and do what is best for *you* in every area of your life—without feeling guilty about it. Think of it this way: If you won't look out for yourself, who will?

3. Your confidence will increase.

You'll be proud of your accomplishments and realize what an incredible person you are. As you shift your attention to your great qualities and recognize how valuable you are, you'll realize you deserve the best and will require others to treat you with respect.

4. You will make it a priority to achieve your dreams.

Self-love, a strong belief in yourself, and unyielding determination will be the contributing factors that bring your dreams to fruition!

5. You will attract loving situations and people in your life.

Your thoughts and emotions attract "like unto itself." If you are thinking loving, positive thoughts about yourself, you will draw affectionate, optimistic individuals and circumstances to you.

6. You will make healthier choices for yourself.

When you really care about how you feel, you'll do whatever is necessary to keep your body functioning at its optimal level. This includes eating healthy foods, exercising, drinking plenty of water, and getting the rest you need.

7. Other people won't have the power to offend you.

As Wayne Dyer once said, "One of the highest places you can get is to be independent of the good opinions of other people." You can disconnect from the energies directed your way that don't resonate with you, and connect only with the energies that make you feel good!

8. You will be happy for others instead of resenting them.

You will delight in other people's successes, instead of saying, "Why not me?" Knowing that you are also able to accomplish amazing things in your life, you'll share others' enthusiasm and will be genuinely proud of their triumphs.

9. You will be of greater service to others.

When you are happier, you'll have so much more to give to those around you. You won't be serving out of obligation, but rather because you'll sincerely *want* to help to make their lives better.

10. You will create your own positive situations and understand that you are not a victim.

As Concept 20 states: *You are a co-creator with God and need not be a victim of external circumstances.* When you love yourself, you won't allow yourself to be involved in negative situations because you'll always strive to feel *good*. You'll engage in uplifting events; you'll surround yourself with loving, positive people; and you won't allow anything or anyone to affect you.

11. Your mind, body, and spirit will be healed.

You'll clear away self-deprecating thoughts. You'll do whatever is necessary to maintain a healthier body. You'll practice techniques such as meditation to create inner peace. *Every* part of you will resonate with the perfection of the Divine within you, and your spirit will soar!

12. You will strengthen your ability to feel your connection to God and to the We Consciousness.

When you practice self-love, you will raise your vibration so that it will be more on par with the pure energy of God. At this higher level of consciousness, you'll clearly feel your connection to everyone and everything.

Be Kind to Others as You Are Loving Yourself

Loving yourself means realizing that you are a significant individual worthy of your own love and attention, and treating yourself with the respect that you deserve. It is one of the most important beginning points to creating peace in your life and in the world!

Self-love does *not* mean putting people down or disrespecting them. Remember, others are just as significant as you are. By treating others badly, you are not only hurting them but also yourself. Keep in mind what the We Consciousness is all about: other people *are* you!

It's important for you to honor your own feelings, but it is equally necessary for you to be kind to others as you are doing so. When you are standing up for yourself, do it with conviction, but in a *gentle* way. Be yourself, and let the world know who you are. Just don't tell others what *they* must be. Do you see the difference? It's all about loving and respecting yourself *and* others, too!

Hopefully you now fully understand that practicing self-love is worth your effort. This essential type of love is the prerequisite to obtaining inner and outer peace. In the next chapter, I'll be discussing why it's also essential for you to remember who you *really* are. When you become more aware of your divinity and oneness with all, you'll be able to love yourself and everyone else on an even deeper level!

CHAPTER 6

REMEMBERING WHO YOU ARE

We are not human beings in search of a spiritual experience. We are spiritual beings immersed in a human experience.

— DR. WAYNE W. DYER

You are not just a physical body; the essence of who you are lives *inside* of your physical body. Stated a different way, Concept 13 says: *You are an infinite spiritual being having a temporary human experience on this planet.* This is not something I simply believe; rather, this is something I *know* without a doubt. In all the years I've been connecting with angels, ascended masters, and deceased loved ones, I have absolute proof of this important concept. I've received messages from tens of thousands of deceased loved ones who have come through during readings. When these messages are confirmed to be true by their living loved ones (messages with details that only the deceased and living loved ones would know, loved ones' personalities coming through exactly as they were when they were here on Earth, messages resulting in items being found, unexpected events that are predicted by deceased loved ones that eventually come to pass, and so much more), then we can easily accept the truth that their souls have survived the death of their physical bodies!

Your spirit doesn't begin and it doesn't end, and this life is just a brief, temporary existence. After you make your transition, you will be reunited with all of the members of your family, friends, and pets who have passed before you. Once you are there, you will go through a life review where you'll be able to see how you have affected each person, animal, and all of nature as well, as if you *are* each of them! You'll be able to do this because you always *have* been everyone and everything else—but you couldn't fully grasp this fact because your physical body had disconnected you from them! As Concept 9 of the We Consciousness states: *After you leave this world, you always feel this connection with the whole because your body is not separating you from everyone or everything else.*

Let me explain the continuation of your soul in a different way. As you probably learned back in science class, energy doesn't begin and it doesn't end. Therefore the energy of who *you* are will always continue to exist. On one of my daily walks when I was first receiving messages from Wayne Dyer, he showed me an image of a huge, blown-up balloon being punctured with a needle. He demonstrated how the air inside of the balloon escaped and continued to exist, even though the balloon was no longer encasing it. He went on to explain that this is exactly what happens to the soul after the body dies; it continues to be present and is free, and goes on to a more loving, higher level of consciousness. It is at this point where you fully become aware of your oneness with God and everyone and everything else.

Recognizing Your Divinity

Not only are you a spiritual being having a human experience, but you also have God within you, which makes you Divine! According to Concept 3: *The true essence of who you are is God. To say it in a different way, God is within every one of us—with no exceptions.*

Again, you will understand this concept completely after you leave this physical plane, but for now, it's essential to reclaim your power and remember who you are. As Concept 4 states: *You are able to easily and effortlessly create miracles in your life and in the lives of others.* For one thing, if more people were able to fully recognize their divinity, then peace on Earth would finally become a reality. After all, God, who is only love, would *never* hurt anyone else or destroy the planet that he created! We would all live in harmony with each other; and love, instead of hate, would be the dominant vibration on Earth.

You Are a Co-Creator with God!

Let's take this a step further. Since you have God within, you have the power to create all good things in your life, including inner and outer peace, regardless of what is going on in the world around you! This is stated perfectly in Concept 20: *You are a co-creator with God and need not be a victim of external circumstances.*

Quiet your thoughts and go within to see what is necessary to create heaven right here on Earth. Then focus all of your energy on assuming the feeling of this magnificent peace. If your dominant thoughts and feelings are those of tenderness and harmony, you will attract more circumstances with this same type of vibration in your life. According to Concept 21: *How you feel about what-ever you are observing creates circumstances in your life that will generate similar types of feelings within you. Therefore, in order to maintain inner peace, you must make a conscious effort to focus on the positive and disconnect from whatever is creating bad inner feelings.*

And finally, as Concept 5 says: *God is only love and peace; you must* be *love and peace to fully feel your connection with him.* You must be Godlike in order to feel him and then extend this wonderful energy out onto others. You can begin by choosing to focus on your many blessings and the perfection of all there is, or as Concept 10 says: *It is imperative to focus on what is right in the world, instead of what is wrong.*

So What Is Your True Purpose on Earth?

Many of my clients who already acknowledge their Divine, spiritual essence still yearn to know what their true purpose here on Earth is. I explain it to them this way: We all come here with different gifts and passions. Some are musically or artistically inclined; others are exceptional in the sciences. Some are amazing speakers; others are guided to devote their lives to taking care of their children and family. The list can go on and on. You'll be able to determine your life purpose by direct-ing your focus on what your true passions are—the ones that make you feel complete, utter joy and a deep sense of fulfillment after you do them. Then, after acknowledging what they are, make sure to share these unique gifts with all those who will benefit! After all, as Concept 32 says: *It is in giving that you receive.*

With all this said, according to Concept 31 of the We Consciousness: *Your true life's mission is to spread the love that you are.* Your real purpose is to spread your unique light with all those you encounter in life—whether it is with your family members, friends, acquaintances, or any member of the animal kingdom. When you share your love and beautiful gifts with others, you will uplift the vibration of the entire planet!

Remember, You Are Part of the Whole

As I previously stated in Chapter 3, we are all connected, and you are just one piece of the total puzzle. Whatever you do to yourself or another affects the whole! God is not only within you, but also within all others!

When you treat yourself with the respect that you deserve, the entire world benefits. Whenever you extend your kindness to another person or nonhuman animal, *everyone* is uplifted. Peace on Earth will easily and effortlessly become a reality when more of us fully understand that we are all one!

In the next chapter, I'm going to show you how to raise your vibration so that you'll be more on par with Source energy. After returning to the higher energy of your true Divine self, you'll never want to go back to living at a lower level of consciousness!

CHAPTER 7

RAISING YOUR VIBRATION

God is a sound frequency, and we can all tune in if we just listen. Some find The Rhythm through different melodies, but it's all music.

— JENNIFER SODINI

We all resonate to a different vibration—some closer to our Source, others further away. The points from which we are resonating attract more situations similar to those vibrations. Although we may be able to hear information from a different signal, the messages will be unclear to us. Those who are further away from the light will be tuned in to negative experiences, such as anger and violence. Those who are tuned to love and compassion will hear mostly that. Those who are tuned in between the two signals will be able to hear and resonate with both.

Abraham (a group consciousness from the nonphysical dimension channeled by Esther Hicks) says it perfectly: "You are perceptual beings with different vantage points and—it does not matter how much information is given—you cannot see beyond the vibrational limits of where you are standing. You cannot live or see or experience outside of your own individual beliefs."

So if we want peace on Earth, we should begin to demonstrate to anyone who is interested *how* to tune in to the higher vibration of love. Show them gently that when you turn on the light, the darkness goes away. Explain that if they want peace in their lives and in the world, they have to *be* loving and peaceful. Make it clear to them that violence will only create more aggression, anger will create more rage, negativity will create more of the same, and so on . . .

As you attempt to explain and demonstrate all this, always try to see through the eyes of others, even if you don't agree with them. Only then will they feel understood! Hear them out. Allow them to be themselves, with no judgment. Let them know your point of view in a loving and gentle way, but never impose or force your opinion on them.

This entire course of action will produce warm, positive results and will bring them back to their natural, loving state. At this point, they will enjoy being in this higher vibration and will most likely choose to tune in to this peaceful frequency more often!

Raising Your Vibration Back to Its Natural, Loving State

Of course, before you can show others how to raise their consciousness, you will also need to elevate your own vibration back to its true, positive condition. The following are some of the many ways to make this happen. Be patient with yourself as you go through these processes. When you master all these techniques, not only will you be uplifted, but also the energy of the planet will be raised!

There's no need to overwhelm yourself by trying to implement them all at once. You can immediately do the first two processes easily enough, but then take your time with the others. You can do them in the order that they appear in this book, or you can do them in whatever order speaks to you. Consider choosing one to master every few days, perhaps one a week; then move on to another whenever you feel ready.

When you master all these techniques, not only will *you* be uplifted, but the energy of the planet will be raised as well!

- **Begin by announcing to the universe your desire to raise your vibration.** Before you get out of bed every morning, proclaim to God, your higher self, and the angels that you wish to elevate your energy. Setting this intention to raise your vibration is the first step toward making *everything* happen!

- **Ask to become a vehicle of love and service.** When you ask God to use you as an instrument of peace, he will quickly send you the right people, situations, and even thoughts that will guide you toward what to do next to attain your goal. In other words, when you ask, "How may I serve?" God will instantly respond with, "How may *I* serve *you*?"

- **Monitor your inner dialogue.** Set the intention of thinking more positively. Remember, the feelings associated with what you are thinking are attracting events that trigger the same sensations in you. Therefore, it's important to direct your attention to the love around you and the peace you wish to manifest in your life, and take your focus off what's going wrong. Begin to clear negative emotions you may be carrying around with you, including guilt, arrogance, fear, anger, and jealousy. These emotions interfere with your spiritual growth and block your special light.

- **Pray and meditate daily.** Praying is talking to God and the angels. Meditating is quieting your thoughts so you'll be able to hear them. As in any relationship, one must listen as well as speak.

  You may wish to create a sacred space to make this practice even more meaningful. For example, you may choose to light a candle, turn on some soothing music, sit in a tranquil spot in nature, or anything else that makes this feel good to you.

- **Practice forgiveness.** As Concept 18 says: *Forgive and ask for forgiveness. When you forgive others, you forgive yourself.* If you hold on to anger, you are harming not only the other person but also yourself. As Wayne Dyer said, "You practice forgiveness for two reasons: to let others know that you no longer wish to be in a state of hostility with them, and to free yourself from the self-defeating energy of resentment."

- **Be grateful.** Be thankful for all the blessings in your life. When you focus upon the amazing things around you, even more wonderful experiences will come to you! As Steve Maraboli said, "If you want to find happiness, find gratitude."

- **Have more compassion.** Become more tolerant and considerate with all those in your path. Treat others with warmth and respect, and send out only positive, loving energy. You will feel uplifted, and so will everyone who comes in contact with you.

- **Eat in a healthy and a more compassionate way.** Your body is a temple of God, so it's important to make a conscious effort to feed it healthy, life-enhancing food. Stay away from refined sugar, white flour, dairy products, and processed foods that lower your vibration. Refrain from eating meat—it imbues your energy with the pain and suffering of the precious, helpless animals when they were slaughtered. When you eat a healthy, primarily plant-based diet, your aura will become so much clearer and stronger, and your energy will be uplifted immensely! (I will discuss this further in Chapter 11.)

- **Empower yourself.** You have the ability to create miracles in your life and in the world as well! The only prerequisite is for you to have confidence in your strengths; be willing to get out there and share these gifts with others. Have faith that you *can* make a difference, and the universe will conspire to spread your beautiful light to all those who will benefit!

- **See through everyone's eyes.** As Concept 16 says, after you die, you will go through a life review where you will see through the eyes of others and know the impact you had upon everyone in your life—both the good and the bad. However, you don't have to die to go through this process. You can go through it now, *before* it's too late. I discuss how to do so in the next chapter, as well as in my book *Through the Eyes of Another*, but you can start this process *now* simply by holding empathy in your heart. Try to see everyone as the Divine beings that they are.

- **Stay away from nicotine, alcohol, and drugs.** All these products diminish your special light. You'll be able to get "naturally" high by practicing any of the methods to raise your vibration that I've covered in this chapter. When you master these concepts, you'll be uplifting your mind, body, and spirit, and won't need any artificial substances to make you feel better.

- **Spend time out in nature.** One of the quickest ways to increase your vibration is to spend time in a glorious natural environment. I know from personal experience that the best time for me to connect with the angels and the We Guides is when I'm outside walking my dog, Duke. That's when I am most able to feel my oneness with everyone and everything, with no artificial surroundings or enclosures!

- **Learn all you can about spiritual principles.** Focus on whatever aspects of spirituality fascinate you, and learn all you can about them! Sign up for classes that interest you or go to the bookstore and pick up books that speak to you. By educating yourself in this way, you'll be plugging into the energy of your true essence and "relearning" what you already knew before you came here in the physical body.

- **Focus on the present.** As Concept 26 says: *In order to experience true inner peace, you must live joyfully in the present moment.* Don't let any negativity from your past or worry about the future prevent you from fully being able to experience this present magical moment.

These are just some of the many ways to raise your consciousness and maintain the peaceful, loving vibration of the Source within you. Remember, you must *be* peace in order to attract it in your life and spread it to others. You can make the world a better place, one step at a time—beginning with increasing your own vibration. As you raise your own energy, you will be doing your part in uplifting the entire planet!

Neale Donald Walsch says it perfectly: "This one simple change—seeking and finding peace within—could, were it undertaken by everyone, end all wars, eliminate conflict, prevent injustice, and bring the world to everlasting peace. There is no other formula necessary, or *possible*. World peace is a personal thing! What is needed is not a change of circumstance, but a change of consciousness."

In the next chapter, I'll be discussing one final exercise for self-love that will help raise your vibration and enhance peace within—writing letters to yourself. Make sure to devote enough time as you work on these letters. Not only will you be bringing all your great qualities to the surface, but you'll also be going deep within to get rid of all guilt that you need to release in order to move on and be happy.

CHAPTER 8

LETTER
WRITING

When you write to yourself, you don't have to worry
about other people's judgment—you just listen to your own
thoughts and let their flow take over. Later, when you reread
what you wrote, you often discover surprising truths.

— BESSEL VAN DER KOLK, M.D.

If you could perceive your life from the point of view of a loving, nonjudgmental outsider, you would have a broader understanding of your life so far. You'd also be able to come to terms with why you did certain things and decide what changes you would wish to make for your future. Even more important, you'd begin to see yourself the way God sees you—as the amazing, magnificent being that you truly are!

A great way to do all this is by writing yourself a loving, compassionate letter. With this process, you will sit down and take all the time you need to reflect on your very best qualities and understand why you responded in certain ways to events throughout your life. When you write, imagine that you are a sympathetic friend, and be sure to maintain an encouraging tone—the letter should be something that makes you feel good.

These warm, positive letters will boost your self-confidence and self-love. This process may be difficult for you to do at first if you have low self-esteem. However, this process is of immense benefit to *you* in particular, and definitely worth the time it takes to get it right. So just be patient and take as long as you need to accomplish this exercise.

The following are guidelines for writing this type of letter. Please feel free to add your own twist to the process, to really make it your own. The bottom line is that the letter is a warm, positive one that will boost your confidence and increase the love you have for yourself.

Tips for Writing a Letter to Yourself

1. Create a comfortable environment for yourself as you begin.

Find a quiet place where you will not be bothered for a while. Set a Do Not Disturb sign on the door, if you need to. Consider praying or meditating to get yourself in the right mood, setting the intention that this will be a positive, uplifting experience!

2. Take the viewpoint of a compassionate friend who is trying to comfort you.

As you write this letter, imagine you are on the outside, speaking lovingly to yourself. By taking a different perspective, you'll be able to see everything in a neutral and sympathetic manner.

3. Start by listing all the reasons why you love yourself.

Mention your qualities that you admire. Spend a little extra time here to write a long list, and give yourself a pat on the back for these amazing traits. Acknowledging your great attributes will help you see yourself in a new, wonderful way.

4. Describe your proudest accomplishments.

Go back through your memory and discuss anything you did that you are pleased with. What have you achieved or what has occurred because of you? Then explain *why* you are so proud of yourself for these activities.

5. Discuss whatever you've done in your life that you regret—then forgive yourself.

If you are dissatisfied with certain things you've done, describe what happened, but look at the events with a new understanding of why you did what you did. To have a better insight on these circumstances, talk about *why* you reacted in certain ways and did these things. Then state that you forgive yourself for each situation, knowing you did the best you could at the time, given your circumstances and the understanding that you had.

6. Write down what you can do differently to make your life better.

Explain that from now on, you will do everything you can to increase the quality of your life. Take note of what didn't work for you in the past. Analyze everything that is not pleasing to you now, and consider what you can do to create more comfortable, happier situations instead. Then make sure to carry out whatever steps are necessary to resolve your issues.

7. Write a paragraph or two to your higher self.

Speak to God within you—the essence of who you really are. Write about how you wish to always feel the true Divine love that is within you and everyone else. Talk about how you wish to reclaim your power to spread peace and to create miracles in the world. Thank this part of you and say how much you honor and love it. Promise to pay more attention to this real you!

8. Conclude the letter with loving, positive statements.

End your letter in a warm and caring way. Sum up everything you said in the letter; reiterate how much you love yourself, why you are proud of who you are, and how you will now take every step that is necessary to improve your life.

Benefits of Writing a Letter to Yourself

This simple practice will enable you to release all the self-doubt and insecurities you've been carrying around for way too long. Because you'll be observing yourself from a higher perspective, it'll be easier for you to notice more of your positive qualities. You'll also discover what changes you should make to improve your life. Use this newfound knowledge to carry out everything that is needed to honor the promises you've made to yourself.

In addition, you'll finally be able to let go of self-imposed guilt and negativity. You'll realize that you did the best you could, given the circumstances.

After You've Written the Letter

Take out your letter whenever you need to be uplifted. Every time you decide to revisit your own special words, you'll be reminded of how much you love, honor, and are proud of the amazing person you truly are!

And because life keeps happening, you may want to write yourself another letter every now and then, especially if anything new comes up that needs your attention. Remember, though, loving yourself is an ongoing process, and you should continue to honor and respect yourself long after you've written your letters!

(For more information on this and other types of letters, you may wish to read my book *Through the Eyes of Another: A Medium's Guide to Creating Heaven on Earth by Encountering Your Life Review Now.*)

You'll receive so many benefits when you take all the steps necessary to love and respect yourself. Writing this type of compassionate letter is just one excellent way to display self-love.

Throughout your journey of loving yourself, always make sure to keep your vibration high so that you're on par with your Divine essence. Remember, honoring your true self is the first step in creating peace in your life and in the lives of others. As Concept 19 says: *You make the world a better place by choosing to be an example of inner peace.*

In the next section, you're going to learn how to extend that love outward. When you show compassion to all others, you will be helping them as well as serving yourself because—as I've stated over and over—*they* are *you*!

PART III

COMPASSION
FOR
OTHERS

Before I began writing the next section, I again asked Wayne Dyer (apart from the We Guides) to give us a message about extending peace to others. Here are my words translating the message he wanted to convey to everyone:

Meditate and pray for peace each day. Ask God how you may be able to serve others. Then be the peace that you wish to see in the world. When you become the peace that you desire, you will attract guidance from above showing you how to serve others. This guidance will come as intuitive feelings to take certain actions. Make sure to trust what you are receiving and follow up on whatever you are being told to do.

Remember, you won't be able to give peace if you don't have it, so always maintain peace within yourself first. Then extend that compassion and give your love to all those around you. You will receive the loving energy that you are sending out to others many times over.

As I stated when I was in the physical body, if you have a choice to be kind or be right, always choose being kind. I now understand just how significant this statement really is! I am now able to see through everyone's eyes, and I urge others to do the same. When you are able to empathize with all humanity in this way, true healing begins.

Finally, remember that focusing on problems such as violence and war will never create a peaceful world. Instead, assume the feelings of peace and harmony as if they already exist on the planet. Then be grateful for the peace that already is a reality all around you.

I, along with many in the celestial realm, will be working with all of you on this necessary endeavor. When heaven and Earth are working diligently together for this great cause, peace on Earth will finally become a reality!

Now you're going to learn how to share your magnificent inner love with all living things. Because we are all one, it's time to extend this compassion out onto all others and heal the "you" in the "We"! This section will be the true key to your becoming an instrument of peace on this beautiful planet.

CHAPTER 9

EXTENDING YOUR PEACE OUTWARD

Nothing in nature lives for itself. Rivers don't drink their own water. Trees don't eat their own fruit. The sun doesn't shine for itself. A flower's fragrance is not for itself. Living for others is the rule of nature.

— UNKNOWN

As has been repeated throughout these pages, since we are all one, everything you do to yourself or to others affects the whole. This is the foundation of the We Consciousness, and it cannot be taken lightly. So if you want a peaceful world, it makes sense then to spread the love that you are unto all others.

To become an instrument of peace, all you need to do is remember who *you* are and fully grasp the fact that we are all connected to each other. Then you need to align your energy to the loving energy of your Source. When you are resonating back your true vibration, you'll *be* the peace that you wish to see in the world.

So just how *can* you align your energy so that it is more on par with who you really are? The following are 21 simple ways to begin this process. However, don't try to implement them all at once. Take your time, focusing on each one until you've mastered it. You can do them in the order that they appear in this book, or you can do them in whatever order speaks to you. Consider choosing one to master every few days, perhaps one a week, until you feel comfortable with it; then move on to the next when you feel ready.

So, let's get started. By following these guidelines, you'll be doing your part in making the world a better place for everyone.

1. Ask the universe how you may serve this planet.

That's right! Just set the intention that you want to make a positive difference in the lives of others. Repeat the prayer, "How may I serve?" throughout the day. You will see that when you ask how you may serve, the universe will begin to show you what you need to do. You will be serendipitously sent all the necessary people and situations to achieve your goals. It's just as Concept 32 states: *It is in giving that you receive.*

2. Embrace your connection to the whole.

This is what the We Consciousness is all about! We are all one within the chain of humanity. When one link becomes disconnected, the whole chain falls apart. So it makes sense to say that we must embrace, protect, and defend our magnificent connection to the whole.

3. Become peace.

As it says in Concept 5: *God is only love and peace; you must* be *love and peace to fully feel your connection with him.*

Throughout your day and in every situation, especially the difficult ones, ask yourself what a being who is capable of feeling and extending only peace would do. Then respond to all circumstances in that way! Peace will manifest when you fully realize that *you* are the Source of this infinite peace.

4. View everyone as beings of love.

Perceive the perfection of God within others instead of dwelling on their faults. According to Concept 23: *You are not able to change others, but you* are *able to change your perception of them.* What you choose to observe in others will create either peace or turmoil in your life and in theirs.

5. See the equality of all humankind.

The essence of Concept 17 is that we are all equal in the eyes of God. No one is better, worse, or more powerful than anyone else. It doesn't matter what a person's nationality, religion, sex, or occupation is. With this understanding, barriers between others will be removed and unity will finally become a reality!

6. Elevate your consciousness.

Nikola Tesla perfectly said, "Peace can only come as a natural consequence of universal enlightenment." Begin to raise your own vibration by following the steps described in Chapter 7. As you begin to shift your consciousness to a higher level, the entire planet will be uplifted as well.

7. Be on the side of those in power who want to uplift the planet.

While on the phone with Tracy Dyer, I asked her what her dad would say when asked how he was going to vote in elections. She said that Wayne would always reply that he would vote for the person who came down on the right (correct) side of consciousness. I told her I was going to remember that response because it perfectly says it all!

When voting for someone in public office, make sure to vote for a positive, peaceful leader who is serving with the intention of the highest good for all concerned—someone who wants to unite, not divide. You'll always be able to tell the difference between this type of leader and one who wants only to serve their ego. Make it your intention to vote for someone who will uplift and bring the planet together.

8. Envision the world at peace.

Feel it as if it's happening now. Read articles about peacemakers. Imagine leaders of all nations getting together to find peaceful solutions to solve any problems between them. Then direct all your attention on peaceful events that are already occurring around the world. As Concept 10 states: *It is imperative to focus on what is right in the world, instead of what is wrong.*

If more people did this, there could be no more war or violence. All the energy directed toward peace would shift the vibration of the entire planet from conflict to harmony. Mother Teresa had the perfect reply when she was asked why she doesn't participate in anti-war demonstrations. She said that she would never do that, but as soon as there was a pro-peace rally, she would be there. So please make sure to envision and focus all your attention upon what you desire, which is peace, instead of fighting against what you don't want, which is war and terrorism.

9. Understand others and treat them the way you'd like to be treated.

As Albert Einstein said, "Peace cannot be kept by force. It can only be achieved by understanding." Really listen to what others are saying and try to see everything from their perspective, without judging them. Then treat them the way you'd like to be treated—with love and respect. As Jesus said, "Do unto others as you would have them do unto you."

10. Send love in response to hate.

If you respond to negativity by sending it back to the person who has directed it to you, this negative cycle will continue, and you will eventually receive this same energy back. If you send love instead, the negative cycle will end, and everyone involved will feel so much better. The only way to put a stop to the ripple effect of negative energy is to begin a new ripple effect of positive energy. The other person will sense what you've done subconsciously and will cease to feel the need to direct negativity toward you. Try it—it really works!

11. Spread peace in the world around you.

Add to the light, not to the darkness. I cannot stress how important this one is. Post on social media about all the love that is presently going on in the world—and there is plenty of it! Avoid watching or reading negative news, including those posted on the Internet. Write positive, uplifting books, blogs, and articles. Practice compassion with all those in your path. Sing, write, and listen to songs about peace. Paint peaceful pictures. Use whatever gifts you have to spread the love!

12. Treat each person as the sacred being they are.

How would you treat God if he walked beside you? Well, he does! Remember what Concept 3 says: *The true essence of who you are is God. To say it in a different way, God is within every one of us—with no exceptions.*

When you are able to perceive the Divine in each person you meet, every encounter becomes a sacred one.

13. Practice forgiveness.

As the saying goes, "Holding on to anger is like drinking poison and expecting the other person to die." In order to create and maintain peace, forgiving yourself and others may be the most significant action you can take.

When Wayne Dyer was in the physical, he spent much of his childhood in an orphanage after his father walked out on his family. Wayne held resentment against his father for so many years, often obsessing about how he would one day get back at him. After finding out his father had been dead for a decade, Wayne went to Biloxi, Mississippi, to stomp on his grave and tell him off. Then, right after he released all his anger that day, he felt compelled to go back and announce to his father, "From this moment on, I send you love and forgive you for everything that you have done."

Almost immediately after doing this, everything in Wayne's life was transformed. He wrote the book *Your Erroneous Zones*, which became a worldwide bestseller. He stopped drinking, lost weight, and started to attract the right people in his life. By this single act of forgiveness, he went on to become one of the greatest authors and speakers of all time.

When you choose to forgive, *your* whole life will be transformed as well. However, please know that I'm not telling you to condone the negative actions of another; instead, I'm saying to forgive the *person*. Many times, they didn't even know what they were doing. As Neale Donald Walsch said, "No one does anything inappropriate, given their model of the world."

14. Learn energy techniques to help you release negative emotions against others.

You may wish to learn and utilize different healing modalities that will help you get rid of your negativity toward others. Some techniques I've found to be incredibly valuable include the Emotional Freedom Techniques (EFT), the Celtic Weave, Expelling the Venom, and clearing your chakras. Donna Eden discusses most of these techniques in *Energy Medicine: Balancing Your Body's Energies for Optimal Health, Joy, and Vitality.* You can learn about the Emotional Freedom Techniques in Gary Craig's book *The EFT Manual,* as well as in *The Tapping Solution* books and film by Nick Ortner.

15. Pray and meditate for peace.

Every day, take three one-minute breaks to focus on peace. In the morning before getting out of bed, spend a minute *feeling* peace on Earth. Imagine world leaders cooperating to ensure global peace and harmony. Repeat this same visualization at lunchtime and then right before bedtime. The important thing is to feel the peace as if it's happening right now. Visualize hundreds of thousands of angels protecting the whole world. See their light and love, feel their protection, and know they are always working with you to ensure peace on Earth.

Pray every day for peace. Say something like, "Thank you, God, for allowing peace to prevail on Earth." As you do so, *know* that whatever is needed to obtain this peace is happening now. Remember not to beg God for peace— instead, thank God for peace as if it already exists. When you beg, it means that you don't really believe it will occur.

Take it a step even further and create or attend prayer and meditation groups for world peace. Many studies have proven that the number of violent crimes significantly decreases whenever a group of individuals are brought together to pray for the important cause.

16. Practice Ho'oponopono.

According to the Law of Attraction, everything and everyone who comes into your life is there because you've attracted it either intentionally or by default. Ho'oponopono, an ancient Hawaiian healing practice, takes this principle of being 100 percent responsible for all that is in your path to an even higher level. It seeks to correct anything that is not in harmony with the God within you. It's about repentance, forgiveness, loving unconditionally, and being grateful.

All you have to do is repeat these four statements throughout the day: "I'm sorry," "Please forgive me," "Thank you," and "I love you."

When you are saying the first two statements, "I'm sorry" and "Please forgive me," you are speaking to others for whatever it is in you that allowed whatever happened around you. Again, it's about being 100 percent responsible for everything. The last two statements help raise your energy. By saying "I love you," you will begin to feel better very quickly because these words have the highest vibration possible. As you end with the words "Thank you," you are acknowledging that your mantras have been heard, and everything about the situation is being cleansed.

When you do this, you heal not only yourself, but also everyone around you.

17. Think like God.

In order to feel and generate peace, your thoughts about circumstances and other people must resonate with the pure, positive energy of God that is within you. When you are attentive to your Source of power, you'll instantly be able to send love in response to any negative energy. You'll realize that retaliation is not the answer, because that would only give the bad energy more strength.

This doesn't mean you need to stay in situations that are negative just to avoid conflict. It means that you can still send love to others, regardless of how they are treating you, and move on from that relationship. Then, after you have stepped away from a relationship, remember to continue to send loving energy, release all resentment, and allow the Divine within you to guide you through any further difficulties with that person.

18. Write letters of peace to those in your path.

Write positive, uplifting letters to those in your life, telling them anything you feel they need to know. In your letter, you can tell them how much you love them, ask them for forgiveness for something you did or didn't do, or tell them that you forgive them for what they did to you. Do all of this while attempting to see through their eyes how *you* may have affected *them*. This exercise will be an amazing healing experience both for you and for whoever is the recipient of the letter. (You'll find more information on how to write this type of letter in my book *Through the Eyes of Another.*)

19. Practice feeling peaceful, regardless of what is going on around you.

Begin by setting aside two hours each day where you will not allow anyone to disrupt the peace within you. After you have mastered this for a few hours, try it for a full day, and then another. By refusing to allow anyone to disrupt your peace, you'll finally understand that you have total control over the tranquility within yourself. You will see that it doesn't matter what happens on the outside that creates peace in your life, but rather, it's how you *react* to what is going on around you. If you find it difficult to maintain this peace, say a little prayer asking God and the angels to help you.

20. Spend time alone.

Make sure to take the opportunity to occasionally get away from it all and spend some quality time alone. While writing this chapter, I was staying a few days in a cabin secluded in the woods at the Omega Institute in Rhinebeck, New York. I can't begin to explain how incredibly helpful this was to me. I was able to disconnect from everyone's problems for a few days and just write, meditate, and enjoy the present moment. While you may not be able to replicate these circumstances exactly, you are probably able to do simple things such as sit in a room by yourself or go for a nice walk alone in a peaceful environment. It will help you release all the negativity around you and will make a world of difference in helping you to relate to other people when you get back to the "real world."

21. Uplift others without lowering your perspective or forcing them to raise theirs.

Continue to stay on a high, loving vibration, no matter what is going on around you. As you are on this journey of peace, you may draw into your life those who are experiencing negativity and need to be uplifted. Yes, it's important to help them out and to see through their eyes, but don't ever lower your vibration as you are doing so. And don't ever try to force them to raise their perspective if they aren't ready to do so.

I recently saw a wonderful post on Facebook about Bishop T. D. Jakes. When he was a guest on *Oprah's Lifeclass*, he told a story about the differences in perspectives between a giraffe and a turtle. He said to imagine yourself as a giraffe, reaching high and aiming for food on the top of a tree. Then he said to imagine a turtle on the ground as all the people who have tried to hold you down. According to him, the turtle represents those who don't understand you. He finds his food only on the ground, never up in the trees. Bishop Jakes explained that we survive at the level of our vision. The turtle can't reach the heights of the giraffe and can't understand what the giraffe is doing. On the other hand, if the giraffe bends down to the level of the turtle, all the blood will rush to his head, and he will die. Jakes added, "You cannot explain to a turtle a giraffe decision," and "When you are built to be tall, you will endanger your position if you lower your perspective." He went on to say that just because a turtle will never comprehend the need to reach higher, it does not make the turtle bad. That is just its frame of reference.

Others may not be able to see things from your perspective because their point of reference is different from yours. So don't be hurt or upset if others can't understand your higher perspective and are not able to receive the kindness that you have intended.

Take, for example, the birds I feed in my yard twice daily. From my window, I enjoy watching hundreds of them come every day to eat. Even though I have been providing food and aid, they still fly away when I try to walk toward them. Sure, I'd love for them to remain there as I am approaching, but I certainly understand that they retreat because it's their instinct to protect themselves from predators. I lovingly allow them to remain on their own personal journey as I continue on mine.

Of course, there are many other ways to extend the peace that is within you onto all others. I hope that these ideas have inspired you to come up with your own! When you spread your true Divine love onto others, it will create a ripple effect of even more peace and harmony around you.

So let's begin right now to raise the vibration of our beautiful planet. To paraphrase Mahatma Gandhi, "Be the light that you wish to see in the world!"

CHAPTER 10

BECOMING PARTNERS IN PEACE WITH ALL THOSE IN THE CELESTIAL REALM

Make yourself familiar with the angels and behold them frequently in spirit; for, without being seen, they are present with you.

— SAINT FRANCIS OF SALES

Concept 1 states that our oneness also encompasses those in the spiritual realm, which includes God, the angels, ascended masters, enlightened beings from other areas in the universe, and deceased loved ones. However, when you are on the physical plane, you won't totally understand this concept unless you are still or are meditating.

Those in the spiritual realm are much more able to feel their connection with the whole because they don't have physical bodies that separate them from all others. Since there is no division between them and the whole, they retain a much higher frequency than those in physical form, and they are always able to fully experience the complete love that they are.

In this chapter, I'll briefly discuss each of these types of spiritual beings, show you how you'll be better able to feel your connection to their energy, and explain how to ask for their help. As you learn about each of them, always remember that they are a part of you! The only difference between them and you is that they are fully aware of this unity.

Let's begin by discussing God, our Source, the creator of everyone and everything—the very essence of who we all are!

God

Although I already discussed our connection with God earlier in this book, I wanted to touch upon a few more things here. The "higher self" is a reference to the fact that God is within every one of us and loves *all* of us unconditionally. God is total love and light—the creator, the link that joins us all together. Although I use the pronoun *he* when discussing God, in reality God has no gender. I love how British psychologist Robert Holden puts it in his book *Shift Happens*: "When you pray to God you are not praying to an 'it' or a 'him' or a 'her' that is outside of you. Rather, when you reach for God, you are simply reaching for the highest in yourself."

Although many of us think of God in a positive way, some will have negative associations and believe that God will punish them for what they've done. There are people who blame God for negative circumstances they are experiencing in their lives. In truth, when we do something we believe is wrong, we just *know* within ourselves it isn't right. We experience a guilty feeling not because God is judging us, but because we are judging *ourselves*. When we step away from what we truly are, which is pure love, we step away from the true essence of God—and it feels awful. If we do something physically or emotionally harmful to ourselves or others, we also temporarily cut off our connection to the whole.

On the other hand, if we do something considered good—for example, when we help others without expecting anything in return—we experience peace within ourselves. This is because the goodness resonates with God who is within us. When we share or feel love, we experience God more fully and subconsciously remember who we really are. Since we are all one, when we help others, we also feel good because we are, in fact, helping ourselves as well!

In my work as a psychic medium and healer, I often interact with those who have experienced tragedies in their lives. Many times, their sorrows cause them to become angry with God, wondering how he could have allowed them to happen. Still, many of these same people feel guilty over their anger. However, it's important to remember that God neither causes so-called tragedies to occur, nor does he ignore prayer requests.

Everything that happens in our lives is a learning experience for the growth of our souls. Sure, we could learn life's lessons in easier ways, but sometimes we don't listen until there is a crisis. Our souls may create events in our lives, such as illness, to force us to wake up and make changes we wouldn't otherwise have made. For instance, sometimes illness enables us to get the rest we desperately need, make the move we really want, quit the job we hate, or whatever else we need to do.

What I strongly recommend is to be still and ask God to help us understand everything in a better way. When so-called bad things happen, our first reaction may be to blame God and ask, "Why me?" However, throughout all our sorrow and helplessness, God still shines for us and never abandons us. He is always, after all, *within* us. Often, when bad things happen, something good comes out of it in the long run.

We can ask God to let us know what we need to do to get well or make a situation better. Then we need to quiet ourselves and just listen, and we *will* receive an answer. The key is that we need to be willing to accept and act upon whatever is being shown to us. God is within us, but respects our freewill choices. He will never force us to do anything. We have to make the decision to take whatever action is necessary for our own peace as well as for the peace of others.

God will never abandon us. When we need him the most, he will carry us through it all. All we need to do is to ask him to grant us peace and strength in any situation. We may not always understand why things happen now, but after we leave our physical bodies, we will finally understand the bigger picture.

Angels

The angels are very real beings of God's light who are here to shine for all of us. They bring us protection, comfort, relief, and understanding far beyond what mere words can express here.

As messengers of God, angels have a higher vibration than those who live here on Earth in a physical body. Their energies radiate pure love and peace. Our bodies are separate from them—they are not within us as God is—but they are still one with us.

Because we have free will, the angels usually don't intervene in our lives without our permission. If we want help with anything, we need to ask them for their assistance, and they will be there for us. No job is too big or too small. We have everything to gain and nothing to lose if we call upon our guardian angels and the archangels!

Guardian Angels

Guardian angels guide and protect us throughout the various stages of our lives. Many of us have multiple guardian angels, but we all have at least one. As we grow and evolve, different angels may also join the ranks of our guardian angels.

Our guardian angels often come to us simply as a thought, a feeling, a knowingness, or a vision. At first, we may feel that we are only imagining the messages we are receiving. Therefore, we need to ask God to let us know when the angels are truly giving us messages. God wants us to become aware of when his heavenly messengers are really speaking to us, so he will send signs that point to this truth.

Unfortunately, many times we unknowingly cut off communication with our angels because we fear what we may see, feel, or hear. Because of this, the angels will not come to us until we are ready for them. In this case, we may want to pray to God to help us release any fears that are preventing us from connecting with our angels.

At other times, we may feel unworthy and therefore do not call upon them for their help. I assure you that we are all worthy of their assistance! They *are* us! It doesn't matter who we are or what we've done; the angels are there for us. They are not here to judge us, but simply to guide and protect us at all times.

Archangels

The archangels have a stronger, more powerful essence than guardian angels. Your guardian angels are here to serve only you; the archangels are here to serve everyone. While guardian angels are present only wherever you are, the archangels can be with you and all others simultaneously. Since they can be in more than one place at a time, don't worry that you'll be taking them away from someone else if you call upon them. Remember, all you have to do is ask them to be with you, and they will be there.

When asking the archangels for assistance, thank them *beforehand*, showing that you have faith that your prayers are already being answered. If you beg God or the angels, it shows that you don't believe your request will be granted.

While there is no agreement on the exact number of archangels, the following 10 are the most well known.

- **Archangel Michael** is a huge, powerful angel. He is the patron saint of police officers and soldiers. His main role is to take away negativity, and he is able to restore harmony and peace in our lives and in the world. He is often seen by those who are clairvoyant as an indigo light. If you are afraid or are experiencing negativity within or around you, call upon Archangel Michael. A simple request to him could be something like, "Archangel Michael, thank you for taking away all negativity from this situation and for always keeping me [or other person] protected."

- **Archangel Raphael** is the angel who will help heal you or others (except in cases where illness is part of one's soul's overall plan for growing and evolving). As a response to your request, Raphael will show you what you can do to get well. He often allows you to see how your thoughts and actions triggered your health problems in the first place. Clairvoyants generally see his essence as an emerald light. A simple request to him may look like, "Archangel Raphael, thank you for healing [whatever needs to be improved]."

- If you need help in speaking your peace or in communicating your ideas, **Archangel Gabriel** is the angel to call upon. (While Gabriel has been depicted as both male and female, in reality none of the angels have a gender. However, for simplicity, I will use the masculine pronoun here.) Gabriel is known to help authors and speakers find the perfect words for whatever they need to say. Clairvoyants often see him as a copper-colored light. A sample request to him would be, "Thank you, Archangel Gabriel, for helping me to perfectly express myself in this situation."

- If you need help feeling motivated, call upon **Archangel Uriel**. He can aid you in finding and fulfilling your life's purpose. He helps in situations where you may feel helpless, and comes to the rescue during disasters. He is very present to help during times of war and violence. Clairvoyants often see him as a whitish-yellow light. A typical statement to him would be, "Thank you, Archangel Uriel, for helping me create peace in my life and in the world. Also, thank you for allowing me to know what my life's purpose is, and for showing me how to accomplish my goals."

- If you need help in forgiving someone, or you want someone to forgive you, **Archangel Zadkiel** is the one to call upon. A simple request to him would be something like, "Archangel Zadkiel, thank you for helping me to forgive [person's name] for what [he or she] has done so that I may heal."

- If you want to strengthen your relationship with yourself or others, you may wish to call upon **Archangel Chamuel**. He helps bring you closer to others and offers healing if you are depressed because someone has hurt you. You may also ask Archangel Chamuel to be of assistance if you feel lonely or if you are having a difficult time with another person. An appeal to Archangel Chamuel would be something like, "Archangel Chamuel, thank you for allowing [person's name] and me to appreciate each other, and for helping me to release the pain [he or she] has caused me."

- If you are going on an interview, doing a presentation, or going on a first date, you may wish to call upon **Archangel Haniel**. He will be of service to you by making sure everything goes well during these very important moments. Say something like, "Archangel Haniel, thank you for helping my [describe the event] to go exceptionally well."

- If you want to see the beauty in every situation, you may wish to call upon **Archangel Jophiel**. She will also help you with any artistic project. You might say something like, "Archangel Jophiel, thank you for allowing me to think positive thoughts that will create wonderful events in my life."

- If animals, such as your pets, need assistance, call upon **Archangel Ariel**. She also helps with environmental issues. A sample prayer to her is, "Archangel Ariel, thank you for guiding, healing, and protecting my precious pets [or other animals]."

- If you know of someone who is ready to pass away, call upon **Archangel Azrael** to help. He is the angel who escorts those who are passing over to the other side. You can also ask Azrael to bring peace and light to those who have already died. A sample statement to Azrael would be, "Thank you for escorting [person's name] safely to God's total peace, love, and light."

The archangels are God's wonderful helpers who are willing and able to assist you throughout your life. As I said, because of Divine law, they will usually wait for you to request their help before they intervene. When you make a request to them for the good of all concerned, they absolutely will be there for you, helping make your life, and the lives of those around you, so much better!

Ascended Masters and Saints

Ascended masters and saints are spiritually enlightened beings who were ordinary humans in past incarnations. They have evolved and attained spiritual mastery where they've raised their vibration to such a pure, loving state as to have cleared all negativity from their energy fields.

Some of the more popular ascended masters are Jesus, Krishna, Moses, the Buddha, Quan Yin, Lao-tzu, and Mother Mary. Some saints are Saint Francis of Assisi, Saint Anthony, Saint Christopher, Saint Patrick, and Saint Peter. You may call upon any or all of the ascended masters and saints—just like the angels, they will be there for you!

Enlightened Beings from Other Areas in the Universe

We are not the only planet in the entire universe that contains life. While we might be the only planet with life as we know it, we are certainly not the only place with life in general.

In addition to being in touch with the angels and deceased loved ones, I have also been in contact with beings that have not originated from our Earth. Once, while I was meditating, I felt a wonderful, loving presence in front of me. I opened my eyes and saw a small being with huge eyes that exuded tremendous peace. I felt I *knew* this nonhuman entity, and it knew me. It was sending me so much love that I began to cry. It was totally unlike the "aliens" we see in the movies who want to take over Earth. I felt as if it knew so much more than we humans do about peace, love, and respect. If more of us on Earth could only know of this peace, there would never be war or violence again!

Those from other parts of the universe don't always have a physical body, and therefore don't need a "spaceship" to be with us. Just like our deceased loved ones, some are able to come to us in spirit form. Because they aren't encapsulated in a physical body, they are able to be wherever they'd like to be, guiding us to make the world a better place.

Just as there are various types of people on Earth with different behaviors and customs, so it is with the many distinct areas in the universe. Their essence can be of many types—peaceful, warlike, civilized, uncivilized, and so forth. However, if you are on the peaceful wavelength, you will attract only beings that are of this higher, loving vibration.

We may think that those on Earth are so advanced, but could there be other planets even more advanced than ours? I'm not talking about advanced technology, but rather being advanced in compassion, love, and understanding. Can people from Earth really understand what love and compassion are if we continue to fight and wage war?

As stated over and over throughout this book, we are all one. This includes being one with the entire universe.

If we cannot hold ourselves back from the destruction of our own planet, we risk going out and destroying other areas in the universe as well. Those in the peaceful outer dimensions would not allow this destruction to occur, so they have been sending messages to all those who will listen about the urgency of maintaining peace on Earth. If you are open and receptive to these messages, you will be able to hear them!

Deceased Loved Ones

When you make your transition, you will return to the real world from which you came. Life doesn't begin at birth and end at death. Your soul, which is your essence, existed before it entered the physical world; at physical death, this essence will continue. When you transition, you will still retain your personality. In other words, if you are quiet, you will continue to be quiet; if you are loud, you will continue to be loud; if you are funny, you will still be funny; and so forth.

When you pass, you will finally be able to feel your union with the whole. Concept 9 says it perfectly: *After you leave this world, you always feel this connection with the whole because your body is not separating you from everyone or everything else.* Also, as Concept 16 says: *After you make your transition, you are able to see through the eyes of every living being.* You'll be in a place of true perfection and pure love, so you'll be able to perceive everything you did that was not Godlike and understand that at those times you just lost sight of who you really were. In addition, you will be more evolved and will be able to fully experience your "Godliness." As Concept 15 says: *Once you leave your physical body, you are able to perceive everything through God's eyes.*

On the other side, you will be very much at peace and want your loved ones to know that—and will try to communicate with them in any way you can! Since you will be able to fully see the bigger perspective of how your actions have affected everyone, you may even seek forgiveness from whomever you may have hurt. And finally, you will able to see when you didn't treat *yourself* with the respect that you deserved, and understand that you are just as important as everyone else!

Those who have had near-death experiences—that is, those who have been clinically dead and have come back to life to talk about what they encountered—often speak about experiencing this incredible peace, their oneness with everyone, and their life review. I highly recommend that you check out the website of the International Association for Near-Death Studies (www.iands.org), which is full of excellent resources that completely explain this phenomenon. A wonderful book on this topic is *The Big Book of Near-Death Experiences: The Ultimate Guide to What Happens When We Die* by P. M. H. Atwater.

Calling Upon and Listening to Those in the Celestial Realm

Make sure to call upon those in the celestial realm to help guide and protect you. Remember, in reality they are all part of you anyway! Whether it is God, the angels, ascended masters, saints, enlightened beings from other areas in the universe, or deceased loved ones, it doesn't matter! All you have to say is, "Thank you for allowing me to feel your presence now," and then be patient and wait, and they will be there for you!

They will probably speak to you telepathically (in your thoughts). However, you'll be able to differentiate your thoughts from theirs. Your own thoughts begin with an originating thought that will then trigger other thoughts about those in the spiritual realm. A message from a celestial being will just "pop" in your head for no apparent reason.

Make sure to take the time to quiet your thoughts through a practice such as meditation, so that you will be able to hear them. If your thoughts are going a mile a minute, they won't be able to come through to you. One good practice to quiet your thoughts is to focus on your breath. You can do this by counting from one to four as you are inhaling. Then hold your breath for a count of four. As you exhale, count again from one to four. Then hold your breath for four more counts. Continue this whole process for about 10 minutes.

Don't expect to receive messages as you are doing this exercise. You are quieting your thoughts so that you can receive messages from those in the celestial realm *later* in the day. It's like putting gas in the car: you do this so that you'll be able to drive later. When you quiet your thoughts regularly, you'll be more attuned to the energy of those in the celestial realm and will be better able to feel them as they are trying to communicate with you.

Those in the spirit world have a higher vibration than those who are here in the physical plane. Therefore, in order to connect with them, it's imperative that you raise your vibration so it is more on par with theirs. You may wish to return to Chapter 7 as a reminder of the steps you can take to do this.

Finally, make sure to ask those in the celestial realm to give you "without a doubt" signs to let you know they are with you. The signs may come in many different ways; the following are some of the most common.

- You may be sent a bird, ladybug, dragonfly, butterfly, or another animal to let you know they are near. The animal will do something it normally wouldn't do, such as land on you or hover over you.

- A song with the words you need to hear may come on when you're thinking of them.

- A car may cut you off, and you'll notice that the license plate spells out a perfect message just for you.

- They may place feathers, coins, or other unusual objects in your path.

- You may see a rainbow in your darkest hour.

- You may smell flowers or perfume in the middle of nowhere.

- Lights may turn on and off when you are asking if they are with you.

- They may come to you in a dream to let you know they are there.

- They may show you the same numbers over and over. You may see numbers that are significant to you in some way or a set of repeating numbers such as 1111, 2222, and so forth.

- You may feel so peaceful and loved when you least expect it.

The list can go on and on, but I'm sure you get the picture! The key is to look for things that normally wouldn't happen that show up for you at the perfect time. You will usually know that it is a special signal sent from them to you! When you receive a sign from those in the celestial realm, make sure to acknowledge it and thank whoever sent it to you. The more you are aware and express your gratitude for this wonderful type of communication from them, the more they will continue to send you these amazing blessings from above!

Become Partners with Them to Create Peace

Those in the heavenly realm are very willing and able to assist you in creating peace in your life and in the world as well. All you need to do is to ask them to become partners with you for this important task, and they'll join you in helping to raise the consciousness of our beautiful planet! Make sure to include the We Guides when you are doing so, since they are a group of celestial beings dedicated to this very purpose!

Then just become aware of the messages and signs they send you. They may give you gentle nudges or feelings to do certain things, so it's important to listen and follow through with whatever you are being told to do. Throughout it all, make sure to fully comprehend that those in the celestial realm are the higher part of *you*, and you *are* worthy and able to receive their guidance. Be the best that you can be and tune in to their/*your* higher energy. You'll be joining forces with those of the highest vibration possible to make this world a better place for us all!

Now we're going to go back to discussing the physical world to understand why it's imperative to also show compassion for *all* nonhuman living things, including *every one* of those in both the animal and plant kingdoms. Sadly, many humans feel they are superior and have disregarded these segments of God's glorious creation for way too long!

CHAPTER 11

COMPASSION FOR ALL NONHUMAN ANIMALS AND THE ENVIRONMENT

Because we all share this planet Earth, we have to learn to live in harmony and peace with each other and with nature. This is not just a dream, but a necessity.

— DALAI LAMA

How do I even begin this chapter when my whole life revolves around keeping the peace and respecting *all* of life, especially those who need our protection? My primary purpose will be to help you understand that no living thing on this planet is more valuable or important than another. Human beings are not on the top of the hierarchy. We are all one! Please remember this.

I recently saw a wonderful post on Facebook by Anthony Douglas Williams who said it perfectly, "We must embrace Mother Nature. She is our friend. We must never make nature our enemy, for we will surely lose that battle. When Mother Nature calls on you for help, listen to her. Take care of all living things, from the largest ocean, to the smallest creature."

I am hoping that you will fully understand that we must all learn to never inflict unnecessary suffering on *any* living thing on this planet. When we do so, not only are we harming them, but we are hurting ourselves as well. As Concept 7 states: *All animals are part of the We Consciousness. To treat them with disrespect is to disrespect yourself because they are one with you.*

I'll begin this important topic by discussing how we can all love, protect, and live in peace and harmony with all nonhuman animals on this planet. Then I'll go on to describe how to do this with all of nature as well. Again, remember, the bottom line is that they truly are one with us!

Living in Harmony with Nonhuman Animals

All life is sacred. Living a life of compassion and nonviolence includes loving and protecting *all* sentient beings, *especially* those who are defenseless and have no voice. To kill, disregard, or inflict pain upon any of God's creatures is a form of bullying. Each and every animal on this planet has as much right to be here as you and me. My wish is for everyone to open up their hearts to all these beautiful individuals and see through their precious eyes.

As humans, we are just one of a colossal number of life-forms on this planet. Through the international research project known as the Census of Marine Life, we can estimate that there are 8.7 million different species on Earth—6.5 million species on land, and 2.2 million in oceans. Furthermore, researchers estimate that we humans have yet to discover 86 percent of all species on land and 91 percent of species in the oceans.

Given this abundant diversity, how can we continue to believe that all these other species are here for our personal consumption and enjoyment? We are not in the wild, where we have to kill animals in order to survive. We have so many wonderful options available to us to fulfill all our needs, so this type of violence is unnecessary. I love the mission statement of Edgar's Mission, a nonprofit farm sanctuary, which says, "If we could live happy and healthy lives without harming others . . . why wouldn't we?"

Love of Animals Includes More Than Our Pets

Many people describe themselves as animal lovers and can easily agree that loving their pets is the right thing to do. After all, *these* animals are our companions. They're cute and cuddly, offering unconditional love and so much more. For the most part, people understand that their pets are dependent upon them, and they gladly fulfill all of their animals' needs. Many treat their pets as their children, and are willing and able to give their "babies" all the love and devotion that they need.

I personally have many nonhuman children that I care for and adore, including two dogs (one of which is blind), two cats, a huge variety of birds (including wild turkey), deer, chipmunks, raccoons, and squirrels. In fact, as I was writing this chapter, I had to stop and take care of all these precious friends and family members of mine. I wouldn't want it any other way!

I could easily devote this chapter to how you can show compassion to the amazing animals in your life. I could talk about finding, adopting, and sharing a life with an animal companion. I'd devote a lot of space talking about how it would be best to first try to locate a pet at a nearby shelter. These animals are in desperate need of a good home, and you would be saving a life if you found one to join your family. While all these are extremely important topics, I have chosen instead to concentrate on all those "other" animals out there that most people don't even consider—those who don't have a name or belong to a human family.

Some animal-rights activists choose to emphasize how badly animals are treated and show horrible videos of their mistreatment. Some choose to throw things at those who wear fur coats. Because of my love for animals (and people!), I understand what they are trying to do— educate people about what is really happening to these precious sentient beings. However, there are many people who can't look at these horrible realities because it is too painful for them. In other words, they can't focus on the negativity because they can't resonate with that. That's because the essence of who they are, like that of everyone else, is only love and light! And because they are unable to face these harsh truths, they don't realize what they can be doing to protect and save these animals.

Therefore, in this chapter, I'm choosing to emphasize the love and compassion for *all* animals and how we can make a difference in their beautiful lives. I'll be talking about the same issues, but in a way that I hope you'll be able to understand better. As Concept 10 states: *It is imperative to focus on what is right in the world, instead of what is wrong.* I truly believe that if I focus on the love within all of us, then you'll be able to fully grasp this important topic better. In order to do this, though, I do have to state some important facts, even though they are very difficult to hear, so that you'll be able to fully understand what is happening to our brothers and sisters in the animal kingdom.

For those of you who resonate with my message here, please follow suit. On social media, make sure to share loving, positive posts of animals and how we can make a difference in their lives. Don't judge or attack those who don't understand because no one will hear what you are trying to say. Remember, it's about seeing through the eyes of others. (I personally am not able to "hear" anyone who is speaking negatively or attacking and only resonate with loving, peaceful messages.) The more we focus on the love—the more love we all will see!

So let's get started. My wish is for you to fully understand that nonhuman animals are part of the whole and therefore are a part of *you.* With this understanding, you'll realize how important it is to include them in your circle of compassion.

Eating with Compassion

An excellent way to begin this peaceful journey is to embrace a vegan lifestyle. Simply put, this is a way of living that seeks to exclude (as far as is possible and practicable) all forms of exploitation of, and cruelty to, animals for food, clothing, or any other purpose. For those of you who haven't tried "going vegan" because you think it'll be too difficult, I'm here to tell you that it may seem like a drastic change at first, but I absolutely guarantee that it'll be worth your effort. Just make sure that your diet is a healthy one. If you can, find a good nutritionist who will be able to show you what you need to incorporate in your daily plan.

As for me, personally, right after my experience with the light that I discussed in the beginning of this book, I began to feel the pain of the animals that I was eating. I just couldn't eat meat anymore, and so I became a vegetarian. At that time, I can't say that I ate a healthy diet. I ate a lot of pasta, bread, cheese, pizza, and anything else that didn't have meat in it. Then about six years ago, I was required to have blood tests done before having surgery to remove a bunion on my foot. The results showed that I had very high cholesterol, which is no surprise, given all the junk that I had been eating! The doctor handed me pills to lower my numbers; however, as soon as I went home, I stored them away in my kitchen cabinet, never took them, and eventually threw them away. Instead, I immediately removed all dairy products from my diet. Within three months of this one change, my bad cholesterol went down 70 points!

I am now a full vegan and have been for many years. I've made simple changes such as drinking almond milk instead of cow's milk, along with eating vegan cheese and other dairy alternatives. There's no turning back for me, and I've never been happier or healthier! (As a side note, I even went off processed sugar and white flour, and my cholesterol has gone down another 50 points, and I lost 10 pounds within a few weeks. Again, with no medication!)

If you decide to adopt this lifestyle, it's important to understand that a vegan diet doesn't have to be boring. Your options consist of numerous fruits, vegetables, nuts, grains, seeds, and beans—all of which can be prepared in so many different and wonderful combinations. You'll just have to be patient and diligent as you learn how to prepare these delicious types of meals, but I know you'll get the hang of it! For amazing recipes and information about how to go vegan, I highly recommend the website forksoverknives.com.

The Reality of the Dairy and Meat Industries

When I decided to go from being a vegetarian to a vegan, I did some research and learned of the horrible conditions of animals raised for the dairy and meat industries. For example, cows produce milk only when they are pregnant, so they must be continually forcibly impregnated. Then, after the cow gives birth, the calf is immediately taken away from her. If the baby is a male, he is killed for meat. (Baby cow meat is known as *veal*.) If the baby is female, she will have the same experience as her mother. The mother cow will be killed for meat at around four years old because that's when her milk production starts to decline, and the costs of keeping her alive and pregnant outweigh the profits she can yield.

As for the egg industry, chickens are bred to lay far more than is normal for their bodies—about 300 eggs per year. (Chickens in the wild lay only about 12 eggs per year.) In the hatcheries, the male chicks are slaughtered immediately after birth through suffocation or being tossed into a meat grinder, because they are not useful. The hens are kept in pens where they are crammed so closely together, these normally clean animals are forced to urinate and defecate on another. Their beaks are cut off so that they won't peck each other out of frustration created by the unnatural confinement.

I can go on and on here about how these precious animals are tortured, but I think you get the picture. All I can say is that if I had known all of this years earlier, I would have become vegan (rather than vegetarian) right away!

For the love of the animals, please give a vegan diet a try. If you feel that you can't become a full vegan, please try to eat less meat and dairy. With each plant-based meal that you eat, you will be saving a precious animal's life!

A Plant-Based Diet for Better Health

For those who wonder if a plant-based diet can fulfill all our nutritional needs, worry no more! To begin with, the American Academy of Nutrition and Dietetics states that it considers a well-planned vegan diet "appropriate for all states of the life cycle," including while pregnant or breastfeeding. Furthermore, many books and documentaries present the copious evidence that support the health advantages of a vegan diet.

In the popular 2011 documentary *Forks Over Knives*, Dr. Campbell, a nutritional scientist at Cornell University, and Dr. Esselstyn, a top surgeon and former chairman of the Breast Cancer Task Force at the world-renowned Cleveland Clinic, present astounding research results that show how many diseases can be controlled or even reversed by staying away from all animal-based and processed foods! Specifically, they advocate a low-fat, whole-foods, plant-based diet. Because of the importance of this material, I highly recommend that everyone watch this film or read any of the *Forks Over Knives* books.

Another excellent source of information about veganism is the book *Crazy Sexy Diet: Eat Your Veggies, Ignite Your Spark, and Live Like You Mean It* by fellow Hay House author Kris Carr. In her book, Kris talks about how she took charge of her health by adopting a "plant-passionate" diet after she received a diagnosis of cancer.

I've also found remarkable wisdom in Anthony William's book *Medical Medium Life-Changing Foods: Save Yourself and the Ones You Love with the Hidden Healing Powers of Fruits & Vegetables*. In this book, Anthony talks about the healing power of specific fruits, vegetables, herbs, and spices. He explains each food's properties, the symptoms and conditions it can help relieve or heal, and the emotional and spiritual benefits it brings.

Just by subtracting dairy from my already-vegetarian diet, I feel so much better! I look younger, I've improved my cholesterol levels, and I lost weight as well. Yet even with all these amazing health benefits, I continue to realize that the greatest advantage of being a vegan is that I'm saving the lives of a countless number of precious, irreplaceable, sentient beings!

What About the Lives of Plants?

The difference between animals and plants involves sentience. Sentient beings have minds, emotions, and desires. Plants are alive, but they don't have these characteristics. What I do know is that when we pick fruit off a tree or other plant, the fruit grows back; we're not killing the tree or plant. And as far as I know, fruit or vegetables don't have familial relations, personalities, or emotions.

If I could survive without killing *anything*, including plants, I would! However, we all have to eat in order to survive. It is important to note here that cows, chickens, and other animals that are being raised for human consumption must also eat plants. So, it makes sense to say that if we take them out of the food system and go straight to plants, we will minimize harm not only to the animals but also to the plants!

Not Interested in a Vegan Diet, or Interested and Don't Know Where to Start?

I realize that not everyone has a desire to become a vegan. When I ate meat many years ago, I didn't want to hear anything about changing my eating habits, so I'm certainly able to see through your eyes. I don't want to impose my beliefs upon you. You may feel a plant-based diet would be too difficult or restrictive, find that it doesn't give you the proper nutrition, or just not wish to change the way you are eating. I'm simply asking that you give it a try—even if it's for just one meal a week. I know you can do that!

For those who want to become vegan but feel it would be too difficult to do, let me say: If I can do it, so can you! In the beginning, even though it may seem impossible, you'll need to be patient with yourself and stick it out! Get all the information you need about veganism in books and on websites. Ask those you know who are vegan for some great recipes.

During this whole process, it'll be important for you to disconnect from your need to conform. Remember, you'll be doing this for *you* and for the *animals*—regardless of the fact that the majority of people still eat meat.

Never force your vegan lifestyle on others. When someone asks why you're becoming a vegan, you can gently tell him or her *why*—for your love of all animals and because it is a healthier lifestyle for you. I promise, people won't give you a hard time if you are gentle in explaining your viewpoint. Once in a while, you may have to deal with someone rolling their eyes when you are ordering in a restaurant. If this happens, remember that it really doesn't matter what anyone else thinks. It matters that you are doing your part in the way you know best to save the lives of animals.

Offer tips only to those who ask and are open to your new lifestyle. Be patient with those who don't agree with you. Bring your own vegan dishes when eating over at someone's house so that they don't have to cook special meals for you. Check labels on all the products you buy to make sure there is no meat or dairy in them. You'll be able to find wonderful alternatives to animal products and will see that the number of places that offer vegan products is rapidly growing!

You may believe that you won't be able to do it all at once. If this is the case, then wean yourself off meat and dairy gradually. I know you'll get the hang of it! When you do, you'll truly understand what I've been saying all along—living a vegan lifestyle isn't difficult at all. As a matter of fact, it's very easy, so incredibly rewarding, and healthier, too! And throughout it all, bear in mind that being a vegan is about being *for* the animals; it's never about protesting against those who are not vegans.

Other Ways to Show Compassion to Animals

Being kind to animals is not just about one's diet. This lifestyle includes being conscious of the clothing we wear, the products we use, and the hobbies we have. Make sure to seek out cruelty-free clothing; most vegans stay away from leather, wool, and silk. Check whether or not a company does animal testing on its products, and read the ingredients in your beauty products, hair and skin care, and cleaning materials.

Stay away from zoos, marine aquariums, circuses, or any other place that keeps animals in captivity. In these businesses, the babies draw crowds and the adult animals are routinely traded, loaned, or sold. These animals end up at auctions, on hunting ranches, or in research laboratories.

Wonderful alternatives to these are animal sanctuaries where people are able to connect and interact with animals in a peaceful, natural setting. I spent an amazing day celebrating Thanksgiving at the Catskill Animal Sanctuary in Saugerties, New York. Because I had sponsored a turkey there, my family and I were invited to attend their *Gobble and Groove* event to honor not just the turkeys residing at the sanctuary but also the 46 million turkeys who are killed each Thanksgiving. At the event, we were given the privilege of petting and hugging the turkeys, pigs, and other magnificent animals, and ate a superdelicious vegan Thanksgiving meal! It was one of the most incredible days I ever had, and I will remember it forever!

Take Part in Positive Causes

Let's begin today to stand up for the rights of *all* animals and include them in our circle of compassion. Sign petitions for noteworthy animal causes, and post blogs and positive messages on social media about protecting *every* living creature. Again, remember to do this in a kind and loving way because no one will listen to us if we are using violent means to attain these peaceful goals. In so doing, our voices will be heard, and we *will* make a positive difference.

As one example, due to the public's outcry against the latest bear-hunting season that ended with 562 animals killed, lawmakers are reviving efforts to ban future hunts in New Jersey. Although the current governor has refused to sign this bill, animal-rights activists are laying the foundation so that it will quickly be approved by the next governor. Jeff Tittel, senior chapter director of the New Jersey Sierra Club, is one of the backers of the bill, which has been called Pedals' Law. The name refers to a bear who often walked upright on his rear legs and was killed during the bow and arrow hunting season.

In another instance, people all over the world voiced their sorrow and outrage when a wealthy dentist killed Cecil, a gorgeous 13-year-old lion who was well known to visitors in Zimbabwe's Hwange National Park where he lived. Because of this senseless act of violence, thousands around the world joined forces to advocate for lions and other animals in the wild. Afterward, many countries changed their trophy-hunting laws.

Because Pedals and Cecil had names and personalities, more people were outraged and became involved, causing new legislation and positive actions to protect these types of animals. However, please understand that there are so many more magnificent creatures that don't have a name or aren't well known. Let's be a voice for *all* those in the animal kingdom. We must join together to protect these precious beings who are not able to defend themselves.

There's a beautiful poem about why we should love animals, attributed to Mother Teresa, that I really resonate with:

Because they give everything, asking for nothing back.

*Because they are defenseless amid men's weapons
and power . . .*

Because they are eternal children . . .

They don't know hate or war . . .

*They don't know about money and only seek
the protection of shelter . . .*

*Because they explain themselves without words,
because their eyes are as pure as their souls . . .*

*Because they don't know about envy or grudges
and forgiveness comes natural to them . . .*

Because they love with loyalty and truthfulness . . .

Because they recognize and appreciate respect . . .

Because they don't buy love, they just expect it . . .

*Because they are our companions and eternal friends
that never betray . . .*

And because they are alive . . .

*Because of this and a thousand other reasons,
they deserve our love!*

*If we learn to love them like they deserve, for being
creatures that feel, suffer,*

and need us, we will be closer to God.

Veganism and the Environment

Veganism is environmentalism as well! As a matter of fact, probably one of the best things you can do for the environment is to become a vegan. According to John Robbins, author of *Diet for a New America*, the land required to feed one person who is a vegan for one year is one-sixth of an acre; the land required to feed one person who is a vegetarian for one year is 3 times as much as a vegan; and the land required to feed one person who is a meat and dairy consumer is 18 times as much as a vegan. This information (and more) was beautifully discussed in the documentary *Cowspiracy: The Sustainability Secret.*

And that's not all. By going vegan (or simply reducing your meat consumption), you'll be helping the world in the following ways:

- Reducing the amount of waste caused by animal agriculture, which is the leading cause of species extinction, ocean dead zones, water pollution, and habitat destruction

- Reducing greenhouse gas emissions (Animal agriculture is responsible for more emissions than all transportation combined.)

- Saving 1,000 gallons of water for every gallon of milk you no longer consume

- Saving 1,100 gallons of water, 45 pounds of grain, 30 square feet of forested land, 20 pounds of CO_2 equivalent, and one animal's life *every day* you lead a vegan lifestyle

To learn more, please watch the film *Cowspiracy* or visit the website www.cowspiracy.com. Also, if you go to www.thevegancalculator.com, you'll be able to see for each year that you are a vegan just how many animals' lives, how many gallons of water, how many square feet of forest, how many pounds of grain, and so much more that you will have saved! You will truly be amazed!

Please consider becoming a vegan or reducing the amount of animal products you consume. You would not only be saving the lives of countless animals but also significantly contributing to saving the environment as well!

Other Ways to Live in Harmony with Nature

Each one of us needs to take the responsibility of maintaining and protecting our beautiful planet that has been entrusted to our care. Global warming, pollution, extinction of animals and plants, and deforestation are real issues that we must take seriously. Very few understand how essential it is to change our lifestyles right now for the sake of our future generations. As we have been concentrating on short-term gain, we have failed to realize that we are totally dependent upon the trees, air, and water in order to survive.

However, instead of focusing on what we've done wrong in the past, let's choose to emphasize what we can do now *for* our glorious planet. If you don't know how to begin, ask those in the celestial realm to show you the steps you can take to protect and support the environment. Then all you need to do is listen to what they say. Their messages will come as thoughts or "gut feelings" to take some kind of action. Some simple examples may be similar to these:

- drive an electric or more fuel-efficient car, such as a hybrid
- use solar panels on your home
- purchase products that are safe for the environment and are cruelty-free
- make an effort to drive less and walk or use public transportation whenever possible

- stay away from bottled water
- recycle everything you can
- deliberately use less water
- don't purchase disposable products (such as paper plates and cups, forks, knives, and spoons) except when absolutely necessary
- avoid buying leather products, including the seats in your automobile, shoes and accessories
- use biodegradable goods as much as possible
- plant trees instead of cutting them down
- practice composting
- and of course, live a vegan lifestyle

You can also speak up and make your voice count for environmental causes. Here are some examples of what you can do:

- **Sign petitions and campaign for more positive legislation.** For instance, if a company is contaminating the environment or producing toxic waste, seek to join forces with others demanding that its factories reduce the amount of pollution they are emitting into the water and air.

- **Speak up to protect our planet from anything that is harming the environment.** Blog about these issues, make people more aware of them on social media, and incorporate information in newsletters. One particular area of concern is fracking, a process of extracting oil or gas that causes methane and air pollution, contaminates the water, harms land and marine animals, releases toxic chemicals, and can even cause earthquakes!

- **Join together with others in marches or other peaceful ways to show your support for environmentally friendly causes.** A wonderful illustration is how, in 2016, thousands came together with the Native American Standing Rock Sioux Tribe to oppose the Dakota Access Pipeline, a $3.7 billion investment to move 470,000 barrels of domestic crude oil a day through four states. These activists wanted everyone to know that they were not protesting at all; instead, they were *protecting* their sacred land and the environment.

Go within yourself and see if any of these suggestions resonate with you. You may also think of something you can do that I haven't listed. It doesn't matter what it is—just set the intention to love and protect our beautiful planet, and ask yourself and those in the celestial realm, "How may I serve the environment?" You'll most certainly receive guidance as to what to do next.

Please don't think that you won't be able to make a difference because you are only one person. If each of us did our own part, we'd finally be able to uplift our glorious planet back to its original state of love and perfection!

PART IV

SUMMING IT UP WITH MESSAGES FROM WAYNE DYER

In this next section, I'm going to share the messages I have received from Wayne Dyer about the remaining concepts of the We Consciousness, the afterlife, and even some unrelated information he has shared with me throughout the year. Although he stated that he entrusted me to write the majority of this book with the knowledge and understanding that I have attained over the years, along with the help of the We Guides (of which he is a part), he now wants *his* voice to be singularly heard!

CHAPTER 12

WAYNE DYER
SPEAKS

THE AFTERLIFE, WE CONCEPTS,
AND OTHER MESSAGES

*It isn't enough to talk about peace. One must believe in it.
And it isn't enough to believe in it. One must work at it.*

— ELEANOR ROOSEVELT

Now Wayne is ready to come through to discuss the afterlife, the remaining concepts of the We Consciousness, and other messages he shared with me. He's *very* excited to spread the news about everything he has learned now that he has left his physical body.

I felt the simplest way to share his information was to ask him questions and then type out his responses. The questions I asked him were spread out throughout several weeks because he "didn't want to be limited to remaining in one point in time and space for too long." In other words, he has been thoroughly enjoying being free to explore the universe and didn't want to be tied down for an extended period of time!

This intimate time I had with him has been such an amazing experience, and I hope you benefit from it as much as I did. The following is the conversation we had together.

Why do you come through when I'm giving messages for your family, but when I was trying to reach you for words within this book, you chose to come through only as part of the We Consciousness?

I am now able to feel my connection with the highest, purest, loving component of the We Consciousness. When I merge with the totality of all there is, I am no longer attached to my ego state. Why would you want to hear from me from such a limited viewpoint for the vital message of peace on Earth? It is in the best interests of everyone to receive this information from the grandest perspective.

But you are still able to come through for your family, friends, and those who have followed you. How is that possible?

The part of me that was known as Wayne will always continue to exist and be connected to my family, friends, and even those who have followed me. And as my family members have noticed, I still have the same traits that I had when I was in the physical body. *[laughing]* They wouldn't want it any other way!

Why do you sound like me when I am interpreting your messages?

You interpret the messages you receive, so they come through in the way you speak. Just as you do in your readings, you translate the details you receive from your frame of reference. If someone else channels us, the message will be the same, but in different words.

As Wayne Dyer, you are also giving many signs and coming in dreams to so many people (myself included). Thank you!

I loved receiving signs when I was on Earth, so I take pleasure in giving them to my loved ones and all those who ask for them to demonstrate I am still here. And, as many know, I can be very creative in the signs that I give!

If your family, friends, and followers call upon you for guidance, will you be able to help them?

Yes, I send solutions into the minds of loved ones who ask for my help. It's up to each person to listen to what I am saying and understand that I am speaking to them in their thoughts. I am also able to come as thoughts in the minds of those who are *acquainted* with anyone who has asked for my guidance, and show each of *them* how they can help these loved ones as well.

Why can't I feel you all the time?

If I come as Wayne Dyer, the person, I can only be in one place at a time. I have done so to be with members of my family as they went through various life experiences. However, when I come through as part of the We Consciousness, with just a thought, I can be with *all* those who wish to speak to me. Raising one's vibration is also a prerequisite for anyone who wishes to connect with me or any other being who has emerged into the nonphysical. When you are not in a good-feeling place, chances are that you won't be able to hear me.

In addition, as I've been telling you many times, "You have to get out of your own way." You won't be able to hear me if your mind is cluttered with your own thoughts. On occasion, my messages were not consistent with your beliefs; therefore, you questioned what I was saying. But you have not done that with your We Guides. You are always able to hear directly from them because their messages consistently resonate with the God within you.

Wait a minute! That sounds like your personal messages do not always resonate with the God within me. How can that be?

[laughing] The Wayne that you know from my lectures and books was sometimes different from the Wayne that I was in my private life. I occasionally behaved unconventionally and had some quirks, just like everyone else. You didn't believe that was possible because you put me on a pedestal, so you discarded some of the unusual messages that I gave you. However, when you've given these types of messages to my family members and other loved ones, it always confirmed for them that I was really coming through.

Will everyone be able to hear your messages?

Anyone who resonates with my words and energy will be able to hear me. I'll be communicating from the elevated frequency of the We Consciousness and will continue to give signs to prove I am reaching out to them.

And, as I already mentioned, for my family and loved ones who knew me, I will still continue to come through with the same traits I had when I lived in the physical body.

Tell those who wish to hear me better to remain in a purer level of consciousness so that their energy is more on par with the energy of where I am now.

What is it like in the afterlife?

Where I am now is not "the afterlife," but the *continuation* of life, without the restrictions of the physical body that bound me to the Earth plane. One minute I was confined to a physical shell; the next I was free as I stepped into this pure state of infinite love. I'd yearned to reach this level of awareness for the last several years of my earthly existence, so I was surprised and delighted to achieve this goal in an instant. As I reentered this familiar state of consciousness and arrived at my true place of origin, I was greeted by my loved ones (including my mother and, yes, my father, too!) and glorious celestial beings, eager to welcome me back home.

I am elated that I can now be wherever I wish to be with a simple thought of a desired location *anywhere* in the universe. I am still aware and interested in what transpires on Earth, but I now comprehend that it is just a tiny speck in the totality of all of creation.

Make sure to tell everyone that the same loving consciousness that you have called God really does exist! It is present within everything and everyone in the entire universe. This spirit of God does not judge me or anyone else because it is all loving. On the other hand, I am now able to see how my actions, good and bad, have affected all those in my life, and I continue to grow and evolve. I am also able to see through my loved ones' eyes to understand why they have behaved in certain ways, with no judgment.

In this new place of reality, one always experiences pure joy and contentment.

I continually bask in complete unconditional love, feeling my connection to the whole, while at the same time experiencing the freedom of doing whatever I wish to do and being wherever I desire to be.

While on Earth, I was able to connect to millions of like minds who were yearning for the truths of which I spoke. To them, I am pleased to say that the essence of the teachings I gave when I was in the physical body has now been confirmed to be true.

Also, please spread this message to everyone who will listen: We are all one in love—everything else is just an illusion.

You have pretty much confirmed Concepts 15 and 16 of the We Consciousness: *Once you leave your physical body, you are able to perceive everything through God's eyes,* **and** *After you make your transition, you are able to see through the eyes of every living being.*

Yes, that is correct!

I'd also love to discuss with you the concepts of the We Consciousness that I didn't incorporate in the preceding chapters. To begin, please expand on the meaning of Concept 2: *Your becoming an instrument of peace is vital to the survival of the planet.*

Everyone must do their part at this critical time in order to ensure the Earth's continued existence. If individuals continue to partake in selfish motives that harm others and persist in living the way they have been, overlooking the effects of their actions upon the whole, then the Earth as you know it will cease to exist. Yet rather than being ingredients of the problems of the world, each of us can become a contributor to the solutions to heal, protect, and ensure its survival. The vibration of the entire planet is raised exponentially whenever another person becomes an instrument of peace. Become a channel of love, and change the world!

As Concept 8 says: *Our individual bodies create the illusion of separation from the whole.* **Now that you have left your physical body and see the bigger perspective, can you offer some words of wisdom about this?**

When I was in the physical body, I had a limited viewpoint: from the awareness of my own personal experiences and surroundings. I knew we were all one, but I understood this only in theory—not experientially. Although my intention was to be of service to the world, I sometimes needed to release my ego to do so, and this wasn't always easy. Now I am no longer in a physical body that separates me from everyone else, so I am always able to feel this wonderful expanded reality of oneness and see everything from this broader perspective.

Please help us to understand Concept 11: *At any particular time, the dominant vibration of the mass consciousness strongly affects what is happening in the world. Therefore, it is imperative that more people become aware of their connection to the whole and are at peace.*

When more and more events occur in the world that are not of a positive nature, it is because most do not remember that they are a part of the whole. You'll be able to tell when the scale has tipped in this direction.

The majority of people will focus their energy on "what's in it for me," disregarding how their actions are affecting others. The masses will act out angrily, becoming blind to the needs of others and indifferent to helping them. They will vote for those in power who are hostile, and choose division over unity. Unless the scales shift back to the energy of love, this negativity will continue to harm the planet.

At this time, those who *remember* they are one with all must step forward to remind those who have forgotten. As more people begin to recall their connection to others and live in a more positive way, the vibration of the entire planet will be raised, and peace will dominate the world.

Then Concept 12 makes perfect sense: *When most people are unable to feel their connection with God and everyone else, world events occur that are not of a peaceful nature. Since we* **are** *peace, we do not resonate with these negative events when they happen. Yet the power of light will defeat the power of darkness every time!* **Can you expand on this?**

When the majority of the population feels isolated and disconnected from Source and from all others, this dominant, flawed energy acts as a magnet and creates world events that make everyone feel even more secluded. These negative feelings and events do not resonate with the Source within you and make you feel bad when they occur. However, just as a single lit match can illuminate a dark room, if more of you turned on your own light, you'd be able to enlighten and transform the whole world.

Can you explain Concept 24: *Healing occurs when the mind, body, and spirit are at peace?*

Your physical body responds to the dominant energy you are emitting. When your dominant thoughts and feelings are in harmony with those of your Source, you'll easily be able to maintain perfect health. Illness occurs when your dominant thoughts and feelings are not in alignment with the energy of God. In order to be healed, it is necessary to plug back into the perfection of the Divine.

To say it a different way, when your mind is at peace and is focused on the perfection of your true spiritual essence, your body will easily and effortlessly be healed.

This reminds me that your autopsy results had no trace of the leukemia that you once had in your body—so you were able to heal yourself from that!

Yes, that's correct. I knew it all along, so I never had the need to confirm this for me or anyone else when I was dressed in my physical body. I was realistic and expected to be healed.

Why did you then leave your physical body anyway? According to the report, your official cause of death was coronary heart disease.

It was my time to move on to bigger and better things. With a simple thought, I now have tremendous freedom to be and do whatever I choose. I can be of service to so many in ways I never could before. I am now able to come into the minds of millions, showing them how to heal the planet from a much higher perspective. This is exactly what I am doing with you now. If I didn't leave my physical body, I would never be able to accomplish any of this.

Yes, thank you so much for that!

You're welcome. I now see the perfection of when each person leaves his or her physical body. It's always exactly at the right time, regardless of how their death occurred. Those on Earth will not fully be able to understand this, so just tell everyone that regardless of *how* their loved ones passed, they always end up merging with the Infinite, in this place of total love and perfection.

We still have a few more of the concepts that I'd love for you to discuss. Please explain Concept 25: *Expect the best, just as God does.*

Your Source comes from a place of knowing and *expecting* that all will always be well. It never anticipates the worst possible scenarios. When you are as optimistic as the Source within you is, you will *easily* and *effortlessly* generate positive circumstances in all areas of your life.

Concept 27 says: *True faith can move mountains.* That's very similar to Concept 25. What's the link between the two?

With true faith, anything is possible. If you are able to assume the feeling of your wish fulfilled, without trying to figure out *how* it will occur, you'll be able to *deliberately create* whatever you desire. Always expect the best possible outcome, and it will come to pass.

Please interpret Concept 28: *Problems cannot be solved with the same energy that produced them.*

Problems exist only in the mind, and they arrive when a person is vibrating at a frequency that is not in harmony with Source. To continue focusing on what is wrong will only produce more negativity and problems. Solutions will occur when one is in sync with Source energy. At this level, the lower frequencies that generated the problems do not exist, and a person is better able to be in touch with and create what he or she *wants* to experience rather than the unwanted event presently occurring.

Concept 30 is so difficult to understand: *Past, present, and future are all now. Time is an illusion.* **Can you explain what this means?**

After you make your transition to the reality where I currently exist, you'll be able to see that the past, present, and future are occurring all at once. Without my physical shell, I'm able to understand that events do not exist in a linear time line. Everything—the past, present, and future—is all happening *now*. On Earth, the past is just a memory of a previous experience, and the future seems unknown, but this is never really the case. You'll see that these are just different phases of energy, not the passage of "linear" time. Everything exists simultaneously, and your individual point of focus creates your reality of now.

That helps, but it's still hard for me to grasp. I guess that brings us to Concept 33: *These concepts are easier to understand when you remember who you are, from whence you came, and where you will go.* **Can you expand on this?**

When you are isolated in your physical body and unable to push the ego's demand out of the way, you cannot fully experience the totality of all there is. Your point of focus is limited to seeing everything through your own eyes instead of perceiving through the lens of the totality of who you *really* are. You'll be better able to grasp these concepts when you are able to recall your divinity, your connection to the whole, and the fact that you have existed before you entered your physical body and will continue to exist after you are free from its boundaries.

In order to do this, you must quiet the voice of your ego.

Thank you! I would also love to include some of the other tidbits of information that you have given me during the last several months. Is that okay?

Yes, I'm ready!

When you were in the physical body, you often used the words *I am* to define who one is and what one is capable of achieving—as a holy expression for the name of God and the highest aspect of oneself. Yet on my daily walks, you told me it's not just "*I* am," it's "*We* are." Can you explain what you meant?

I now see that "I am" implies that you are not; it isolates you from the whole. When you instead say, "*We are*," you affirm from the perspective of being a *co*-creator with the God within all of us.

Instead of saying, "I am," say, "*We* are." After saying, "*We are*," just add whatever it is you wish to attain: *We* are peace, *We* are Divine, *We* are love, *We* are abundant, *We* are in perfect health, and so forth. Then watch miracles begin to unfold in your life and in the lives around you!

I began this book on January 1st and am now putting the final touches on it the following January 1st. What is the significance of this date?

January 1st signifies wonderful new beginnings. In this case, it is the returning of peace on planet Earth!

You told me that even if the world changed for the better, it would not create the peace that a person desires. What did you mean by that?

What is happening outside of yourself won't create peace in your life. It is your discernment of what is happening that will generate either peace or unhappiness within you. For peace in your life, you must choose to see the bright side of every situation.

You have free will, and you alone have the power to modify what you are thinking and feeling. Neither I nor anyone or anything from the outside world can force you to change your thoughts.

You also told me something I had already suspected: "Those in spirit are drawn to those in the physical who have similar goals and interests as they had when they were still here on Earth."

Yes, that's correct. As for me, I am now able to understand who a person is simply by observing their energy. With the permission of those in the physical, I can also join forces with all those who have a similar energy field as mine to promote our common interests and goals. Everyone emits a vibration that attracts "like unto itself" from the spirit world. By seeing your energy, Karen, I knew you had the same goals as mine. I also knew you could help me communicate with my family.

You told me to stop worrying about what others think of me. Why did you say that?

Being preoccupied with other people's opinions about what you are doing is a waste of your time. Whatever someone thinks of you is a reflection of *their* vibration, not yours. Continue to focus on being of service to yourself and to the world, and allow others to take care of their own energy.

I found it fascinating what you had told me a few months ago about the correlation of intuition and the length of a person's hair. Can you share with us what you said about that?

From where I see now, your hair acts as an antenna and picks up on the energy around you. Having longer hair increases intuitive abilities. Have you noticed that many of the greatest spiritual teachers had longer hair? Also, why do you think women seem to be more intuitive than men? This doesn't mean that you won't be intuitive if you are bald like I was *[laughing]* or if your hair is shorter. It just means that your intuitive abilities increase with longer hair. The Native Americans are aware of this, and it is one of the reasons they do not cut their hair.

On one of my daily walks, you talked about something we should ask our children when they are still young. Can you tell us what that is?

Yes! Instead of asking your children what they want to *be* when they grow up, ask them how they will be able to make the world a better place by using their own special talents. Keep this discussion going throughout their childhood years, and show them that they can make a positive difference on the planet by living their passion!

Thank you. That's beautiful! It's like living your soul's purpose.

Exactly!

On another one of my walks, I became frustrated when someone was coming toward me on the same street and interrupted my receiving messages from you. I loved what you told me when this happened. Can you share this again for all to hear?

Alone time is very important to many, especially those on the spiritual path. However, you need to remember that the other person is also you—and *me* as well! It's important to practice what you have learned about the We Consciousness. We are all walking through life together. We are all one.

Thanks so much for reminding me. Wayne, I wanted you to share one more thing before we conclude. At one point, you showed me a visual of dark energy underneath the earth rising above the surface. Can you tell us what this meant?

At this time, a significant amount of negativity that has been stuffed down on Earth over the last several decades is beginning to erupt from underneath the surface. Do not be fearful, because this is necessary for the commencement of a thorough cleansing of the darkness with the light. Be thankful because the planet is now rising to a new level of awareness.

While many will join forces with the darkness, an even larger number of others will become aligned with the energy of the We Consciousness to heal the planet. Each individual will make the choice as to which direction to take. Make sure to choose wisely and become a channel of peace. Allow the God-force that is within you to shine through.

Yes, of course! That is the purpose of this book—to show everyone how to become instruments of peace. It's almost as if the timing of this book were Divinely planned!

Yes it was . . . But then again, everything always *is*!

Thank you for dedicating your time to coming through for us. It has been such a wonderful experience! Is there anything else you wish to add here?

Just tell everyone to keep my teachings alive and to spread my newfound wisdom! I will be guiding all who wish to continue in my path.

I am alive and well. There is no death!

CHAPTER 13

JOINING TOGETHER IN LOVE

*We are here to awaken from the
illusion of our separateness.*

— THICH NHAT HANH

On August 30, 2015, the world thought it lost one of the most influential writers and speakers of all time. I am beyond delighted that Dr. Wayne W. Dyer, the "Father of Motivation," has proven everyone wrong! He is now able to come through to anyone who is willing to hear his message and is tuned in to his vibration.

My own connection with Wayne began after I repeated the question Wayne suggested everyone ask the universe: "How may I serve?" As soon as I made this request, he was right there, showing me how I could help his family and guiding me as to what I could do to make a difference in this world.

No, our planet has not lost Wayne Dyer at all. It has *gained* his magnificent wisdom on an even deeper level now that he is in the celestial realm. He is now able to help in ways he never could before, and he is ready and willing to be with us every step of the way! As you have seen, he's particularly concerned with maintaining peace on our planet.

I am truly blessed that I am able to hear him, along with the rest of the We Guides, to bring the We Consciousness into your awareness at this significant period in time. Please listen to these profound messages of peace and spread the love. Your service is very much needed, right here and now. Don't wait for someone else to accomplish what *you* have the power to achieve! Use your unique abilities to make a difference in the world.

Please join Wayne, Saint Francis of Assisi, the We Guides, and me in becoming an instrument of peace. Just as each of the five fingers has its own special job within the same hand, as every piece to a puzzle is needed to complete it, and as all the links to a chain are necessary for the chain to remain connected, so it is with every one of us. We all can do our own part in making the world a better place for everyone!

May you plant seeds of love, unity, and peace—first within, and then outside of yourself. Make sure to sprinkle the precious seedlings daily with rays of kindness, and give each sprout all the loving energy it needs to flourish. After you have fertilized your peace garden, make sure to scatter some seeds of compassion as you go along. You may even wish to call upon your spirit guides and angels to help germinate this Divine foliage.

You will reap what you have sown, so make sure to keep replanting only seeds that are of the light. As the foliage continues to blossom, gently weed out anything that comes up that does not resonate with the love, unity, and peace that you have originally planted.

Remember to be patient, for some of the vegetation may develop slowly; never pull anything out by its roots because it may be growing in ways you may not immediately see, deep below the surface! While this whole process may take a lot of time and work, it will truly be worth all of your effort. The tiny love seeds that you originally planted in your small garden will eventually bloom into an abundantly fruitful forest of peace and tranquility. And it will all have occurred because you continued to stay connected to the We Consciousness and became an instrument of peace!

As this book comes to a close, Wayne, the rest of the We Guides, and I wish you a life filled with every blessing that you could ever imagine. May love surround you, angels protect you, and the Divine within you guide you as to what steps you need to take now to be of service to the universe.

We love you so much! May peace prevail on Earth!

APPENDIX A

The 33 Concepts of the We Consciousness

1. The most important truth is that we are all one. Our oneness encompasses everything and everyone, including God, the angels, ascended masters, enlightened beings from other areas in the universe, deceased loved ones, animals, and nature.

2. Your becoming an instrument of peace is vital to the survival of the planet.

3. The true essence of who you are is God. To say it in a different way, God is within every one of us—with no exceptions.

4. You are able to easily and effortlessly create miracles in your life and in the lives of others.

5. God is only love and peace; you must *be* love and peace to fully feel your connection with him.

6. You reinforce your connection to God with positive thoughts and actions.

7. All animals are part of the We Consciousness. To treat them with disrespect is to disrespect yourself because they are one with you.

8. Our individual bodies create the illusion of separation from the whole.

9. After you leave this world, you always feel this connection with the whole because your body is not separating you from everyone or everything else.

10. It is imperative to focus on what is right in the world, instead of what is wrong.

11. At any particular time, the dominant vibration of the mass consciousness strongly affects what is happening in the world. Therefore, it is imperative that more people become aware of their connection to the whole and are at peace.

12. When most people are unable to feel their connection with God and everyone else, world events occur that are not of a peaceful nature. Since we *are* peace, we do not resonate with these negative events when they happen. Yet the power of light will defeat the power of darkness every time!

13. You are an infinite spiritual being having a temporary human experience on this planet.

14. It is imperative to love and respect yourself, and understand that you are just as significant as everyone else.

15. Once you leave your physical body, you will be able to perceive everything through God's eyes.

16. After you make your transition, you are able to see through the eyes of every living being.

17. We are all of equal power and love. One is never more powerful than another.

18. Forgive and ask for forgiveness. When you forgive others, you forgive yourself.

19. You make the world a better place by choosing to be an example of inner peace.

20. You are a co-creator with God and need not be a victim of external circumstances.

21. How you feel about whatever you are observing creates circumstances in your life that will generate similar types of feelings within you. Therefore, in order to maintain inner peace, you must make a conscious effort to focus on the positive and disconnect from whatever is creating bad inner feelings.

22. External objects or circumstances do not create inner peace.

23. You are not able to change others, but you *are* able to change your perception of them.

24. Healing occurs when the mind, body, and spirit are at peace.

25. Expect the best, just as God does.

26. In order to experience true inner peace, you must live joyfully in the present moment.

27. True faith can move mountains.

28. Problems cannot be solved with the same energy that produced them.

29. When you direct your attention to love and light outside of yourself, you expand the light within yourself as well.

30. Past, present, and future are all now. Time is an illusion.

31. Your true life's mission is to spread the love that you are.

32. It is in giving that you receive.

33. These concepts are easier to understand when you remember who you are, from whence you came, and where you will go.

APPENDIX B

The Dyer Family Speaks

As I explained in the beginning of this book, when I received the first message from Wayne Dyer, I wanted a "without a doubt" sign to know it was really from him. That's when I received the sign of the *We* sticker in my shirt. After a series of events, his wife and three of his daughters came to see me in New Jersey, and Wayne came through loud and clear with messages that only his family and he would know. He has continued to give me proof throughout this year by having me contact different family members as they went through various significant experiences in their lives. One of my favorites was when he made me call his daughter Serena at the exact time that she was ready to give birth to her second daughter to tell her that her daddy was with her.

After I had finished the first three parts to this book, Wayne decided that he wished to come through by himself. To prove to everyone that he really is still around, he wanted me to share some of the messages that he gave to his family.

When Wayne comes through for his family, he is always loud and forceful. He repeatedly tells me to "get out of the way" so that I can receive these messages, often at the *exact* moment something of great magnitude is happening with them. Because the majority of the messages he has relayed through me are too personal to share, I will not be including all of them here. Instead, the Dyer family decided to share their experiences in their own words.

Marcelene Dyer (Wayne's wife)

On that day, our family was together for our usual Sunday brunch or dinner. Some of the members of our family were out of town: Tracy was at home in Minneapolis, Sands on a surfing trip in Nicaragua, and Saje was in New York.

When Dee, Wayne's new assistant, called to inquire if we had heard from him, it was around 5 P.M. here, but only 11 A.M. in Maui, where he was. Many of us had been in contact with him within the last 48 hours. About a half hour later, Dee called the hotel manager, and they were able to open his door. Wayne was pronounced dead while we all held our breath, listening on a home speakerphone.

Wayne was gone—or so we thought.

A few months later, we were introduced to Karen Noé. Saje was invited to a special session with her in New Jersey, and she invited me, Skye, and Serena to accompany her. All of us arrived at Karen's studio, and without a doubt, Wayne arrived, too. There can be no mistaking his mannerisms and voice. Karen *became* him at times, giving each of us priceless messages that only he could have brought to her.

Wayne even apologized for things that no one else could possibly have known about. These situations were private; there was no online record she could have discovered. When Wayne came through that day, he was finally able to see through my eyes and understand how his actions had affected me.

All of us were given proof that he was present and had never left. Karen, humble as she is, encouraged each of us to be our own medium and to ask our loved ones to show us they are still with us. From then on, I have had more proof he is always present and loving.

Tracy Dyer (Wayne's eldest daughter)

On August 30, 2015, my father, Dr. Wayne Dyer, passed away. His passing was a shock to our entire family, and the months following this horrible event were incredibly difficult for all of us. There were so many things we had planned, and so many things we still thought we would be able to do. The shock and loss were very difficult to comprehend. For me, specifically, there were still many things left unsaid.

Karen Noé has proven to be a complete godsend to our family. A few months after my dad's passing, Karen did a reading for me, and she shared many specific events and details that she could never have known. I left the reading feeling very connected to my dad again. This kind of connection is unbelievably comforting when you have lost someone you love. Unless you have experienced a serious loss in your life, this is a difficult concept to grasp.

A few weeks after this initial reading, I was participating in a trade show in Las Vegas, Nevada, for my company, Urban Junket. My sales manager and I had spent an entire exhausting day setting up our booth and then grabbed some dinner and gone back to the hotel. We wanted to sleep early so we could get up early to get ready for the first day of the actual show.

At 5:45 the next morning, I woke up quickly from a very intense dream I was having about my dad. It was the first time since he had passed that I had dreamed about him. At 5:46 A.M., my cell started vibrating from a text I had just received from Karen. It read: "Are you ok? Your dad is here and he wants to talk to you now. Can I call you?" I said yes, and she called 30 seconds later.

Karen asked, "What is going on? Your dad is here, and he's really adamant that I call you right now."

I said, "That's so strange because I just had a really intense dream about him. He was telling me everything was going to be okay, and I was pounding on his chest and saying, 'You never listen to me, and if you had you wouldn't have died.' I had been asking my dad to see a cardiologist for years regarding his intermittent shortness of breath, but he always said that he didn't like doctors and that he was in perfect health. My dream was so intense that I woke up crying."

Karen replied, "Your dad wants you to know that he's listening to you now, and he's so sorry that he didn't before. Keep talking to him out loud. He hears you, and he's communicating with you through your thoughts." My dad told me via Karen that his death was in Divine order and happened exactly when it was supposed to. He told me to meditate more often, and he would be able to come through during those times.

These kinds of messages and the timing and intensity of the messages are truly a gift from God, and I am forever grateful to have Karen Noé and her amazing gifts in my life.

Skye Dyer (Wayne's daughter)

When my dad passed away, I felt so lost. I couldn't imagine a world without him in it; he was so big in life that I felt an immediate void. Time stood still for that first month, but eventually I started to remember what my dad taught me about life and death and the bigger picture.

My sisters, mom, and I got to meet Karen in October of 2015, about six weeks after my dad passed away. I used to be a little trepidatious when speaking to psychics or mediums, but I was so excited to speak to Karen—something felt different. On the way to Karen's, we discussed among ourselves what specific things we wanted our dad to answer so that we would know it was really him when he came through. Within the first five minutes of our reading with Karen, she had already blown our minds. When my dad spoke to me through Karen, it was with a gentle voice; when speaking to Serena, his voice was a little rougher. It was exactly how he spoke to us in life! We couldn't believe it.

One of the first things Karen said to me that day was, "Your dad is saying that he comes to visit you as a white bird." My mouth dropped. About two weeks prior, I'd had a strange incident with a large white bird in my backyard. I looked right at it and said, "Hi, Dad." In that moment, I thought I was crazy. But now, all of the sadness I'd been feeling so strongly started to dissipate. I started to know that he really was still here, just in a different way.

One night, about a week after meeting with Karen, I was having a hard time. I was questioning my singing and songwriting career. You see, I had spent my whole adult life thus far traveling and performing with my dad. I felt scared about my future, and mainly I felt alone without his guidance and support.

The next morning I woke up to an e-mail from Karen that said, "Your dad is saying that he is with you, and you have to keep singing. Be fearless; he will still be with you on stage." I couldn't help but smile. You see, my dad always had me write "Be fearless" on a piece of paper before I went on stage to sing.

I could go on and on with examples. Karen Noé is such a gift, and she has helped countless people learn how to heal and understand what happens after someone leaves us. I am forever grateful to her. She always reminds me to stop and listen because my dad is still guiding me; I just have to pay attention. I believe that my dad is helping even more people now than when he was alive. The endless e-mails and messages I receive from people is proof of his guidance. We just all have to start paying attention.

Sommer Wayne Dyer Camp (Wayne's daughter)

Karen Noé is the real deal. Her gift has singularly changed my perception of life after death.

The first time I spoke with Karen she had a message for me from Elizabeth, a college friend of mine who had recently passed away. Karen explained how my friend's father had attended one of her recent seminars, and Elizabeth came through with a message for him and me. Her message was, "Tell Sommer to tell Josh [her ex-boyfriend and a mutual friend of ours] that I was really messed up back then, but I am okay now." It blew my mind that Elizabeth knew that Karen could relay the message to me!

During that first conversation, my father also came through. Karen told me that my father is always only a thought away and told me to be strong, and then suddenly she said, "He's with your horse! Your horse is there!" This completely convinced me. My first horse had passed away when I was 13. This is not public knowledge, and there is no mention of this personal event online or on Facebook. There was no way she could have known that or put any of that stuff together without help from my loved ones who had crossed.

Since that day, I have relayed Elizabeth's message to Josh, and he was so grateful that I did. He said he was now at peace with her passing. I also spoke with Elizabeth's dad, and we marveled over Karen's ability and how our own lives had been changed upon receiving these "without a doubt" messages.

Thankfully Karen has continued to reach out to me each time my father needs to relay a message. It is uncanny how timely they always are. Most recently, I had been spending a lot of time worrying about my health due to some peculiar symptoms. My worry was starting to consume my mind despite having been seen by a doctor. I was relieved when the phone rang, and it was Karen. She said my dad wanted to reassure me that I was going to be okay, but that I did need to follow up with my doctor and take better care of myself. I was blown away! There is no way she could have known that I was worried about my health.

Since my father's passing a year and a half ago, I have had the privilege of speaking with Karen many, many times. Through our conversations, I have finally been able to make some vital, long-overdue changes in my life. I was encouraged and comforted to know for sure that my father is watching and that he's with me every step of the way. I want to make him proud. In a way, I feel closer to him than ever before. Karen has given me peace of mind. Before I thought he was with me, but I didn't know for sure. Now I *know*.

Each time my father has urged her to call me to relay something to me, the message has been spot on. Not once has she been wrong in the delivery of the message. I am so grateful that my father found her, and that my college friend did, too. She has shown me how to pay attention to my thoughts and has explained that my father communicates with me that way. Her gift and her willingness to deliver the messages have changed my life. What she tells me continues to blow me away. I cannot wrap my head around how or why she is blessed with this ability and how exactly it all works. I just know it does work and that even though my dad is not in his physical body, he is with me now more than ever. Her abilities have allowed me to still be in touch with my dad.

Karen has opened my heart and given me the gift of knowing that our loved ones are still with us, even after they die. For that I will be forever grateful.

Serena Dyer (Wayne's daughter)

I walked into Karen's office in October of 2015 with my mom and two of my sisters. Karen started off by saying that my dad was so excited we were there. She was using phrases and expressions that my dad had used my entire life to rush us along whenever he was anxious about getting going.

Karen said right off the bat to me that my dad was saying I was pregnant. I immediately felt a little down because it made me feel like maybe she wasn't the real deal. I had a six-month-old baby at home, and I thought that Karen was getting my current baby confused with me being pregnant. I didn't think it was even a possibility for me to be pregnant again at that time. However,

Karen was adamant that my dad was not talking about my daughter, Sailor, and insisted that I was in fact pregnant again. My dad said that he was with the baby and there was something about fireworks, but Karen wasn't sure what it meant. He just kept suggesting fireworks and the Fourth of July.

During that initial meeting, Karen went on to say such specific things, using such specific words and phrases, and even mentioning dreams that we'd each had that no one else knew about that it became increasingly clear my dad was communicating to us through her. Before my dad passed away, he sat my husband and me down and talked to us about the importance of looking at a crisis we were experiencing as a blessing rather than a curse, and he was also adamant that this crisis was going to bring us even closer together in our marriage. This was a very private conversation between only my dad, my husband, and myself, yet Karen was repeating what he had said to us at that meeting almost verbatim. She was stressing that my dad could see more clearly from where he was, and he was adamant that all obstacles that appear in our lives are really blessings in disguise. It was so comforting to hear Karen repeat his exact words from that conversation, as it gave me the knowing that my dad really was there with all of us, using Karen's gift as a medium to communicate with us what he had already been teaching while he was alive. His personality, his sense of humor, and even his different ways of talking to each of his children came through so clearly.

After our initial meeting with Karen, we were all deeply touched and impacted, but also overcome with a sense of peace and a knowing that our dad was still there with us, just in a different way. Since it became so clear that Karen really was communicating on behalf of our dad, the first thing we did when we left her office was stop at a drugstore for that pregnancy test. Sure enough, it was positive. The fireworks reference? Well, my due date was the Fourth of July! Little Windsor Wayne made her arrival this past July 1, on my wedding anniversary. Sure enough, just as I was about to start pushing, Karen called to say my dad was telling her I was moments away from welcoming our baby girl, and he was right there with me each step of the way. It gave me the calmest, most peaceful feeling right before I brought our daughter into the world because I knew without a doubt he was there. How else would Karen have known I was moments away from giving birth? She didn't even know I was in labor! My dad was even joking with Karen that the baby would be a little angel because of all the time he spent with her before she was born, and so far, she really is.

Karen's ability to communicate on behalf of my dad is truly astounding. I have many more examples of her "without a doubt" gift, and I am so grateful that my dad placed her in our lives. She is a blessing to the entire Dyer family.

Sands Dyer (Wayne's son)

I was at a crossroads in my life, trying to decide whether or not I should follow my dream and move to Hawaii. I decided to move confidently, yet still had reservations in the back of my mind. After traveling for 13 hours from Florida to Maui, I received a call from Karen Noé. She told me that the moment she had returned home from being out all day, she saw an e-mail chain that she and I had written to each other over the year prior. This e-mail miraculously appeared on her screen, completely out of the blue, in the same moment that I had landed in Maui with reservations about my decision to move so far from home!

Karen then informed me that my father came through in a very strong manner (as he tends to do) to tell her to call me right at that moment. He said to tell me that I was making the correct life decision. This message from my father, through Karen Noé, allowed me to stay confident in the direction of my dreams and brought me deep peace just at the moment when I needed it the most.

Saje Dyer (Wayne's daughter)

After my father passed away, I always knew that he was still right here with me, by my side, holding my hand, and embracing me in endless and infinite love. What I did not know was how I could still communicate with him and hear him and feel him in "without a doubt" ways.

Karen Noé has been an immeasurable guide in helping me learn to hear and feel my dad from the other side. She has given me and my family messages from my dad that are intensely personal and precise. I know without a doubt that Karen is communicating with my dad.

On one occasion when I was having a medium session with Karen, my dad was going on and on about a heart-shaped piece of jewelry. I told her that I wasn't really sure what he would be referring to. So Karen asked him to be more specific, and he went on to say that the heart-shaped piece of jewelry was a family heirloom and that there was an engagement coming up for me in the near future. Even though I was still not really able to understand the message about the jewelry, I could feel his and her excitement about my upcoming engagement.

Lo and behold, two months later my boyfriend proposed to me with the heart-shaped diamond that had been my mom and dad's engagement ring many years prior!

I am so honored and humbled that I can be of service and bring Wayne's messages to his precious family, always at the perfect time! He is still with them, as strong as he has always been, and is helping them in ways he never could before. He is also appearing to them, coming in dreams, and giving signs to confirm he is still by their sides. In addition to regularly connecting to them through me, he speaks to each one directly and is happy that they are becoming more aware whenever he is around!

He has also been giving "without a doubt" signs to thousands of people all over the world, proving that he can easily and effortlessly get his message across, just as he did when he was physically here! He was a large presence when he was in the physical body, and is even larger now that he has "awakened"!

APPENDIX C

Peace Prayers

Prayer and meditation are useful practices for deepening your connection with God and everyone and everything. To aid you in your contemplation, I've included several prayers that I've written, two prayers that I've found particularly inspirational, and peace prayers from all major religions. I suggest that you read through the list, then pick one each day to meditate upon.

Prayer for a Deeper Understanding of the We Consciousness

Dearest God, please bring into my awareness how I may be of service to uplift this beautiful planet.

Help me to understand that I am one with everything and everyone, including each member of your precious animal kingdom and all of nature.

Enable me to realize that whatever I do to myself or to another affects the whole.

Allow me to remember that you are within me, and therefore I can easily create miracles in my life and in the world as well.

Help me to forgive all those who have harmed me in any way.

Guide me in seeing through the eyes of others, and in seeking forgiveness from anyone who I may have hurt.

Enable me to treat myself with the respect that I deserve, with the deeper understanding that I am just as important as everyone else.

Assist me in understanding that whatever I focus upon grows energetically.

For this reason, grant that I may continue to focus on peace instead of war, love instead of hate, light instead of darkness, and unity instead of division.

By shifting my focus toward your Divine light, I am doing my part in creating a more peaceful world for all.

And so it is.

Prayer to Create Peace Within

Dearest God, help me to release anything that I am holding on to that is preventing me from experiencing your total peace.

Assist me in forgiving everyone who has hurt me in any way.

Enable me to forgive myself for those times when I have been less than perfect.

Help me to understand the concept that anything besides love is just an illusion.

With this newfound knowledge, show me how to release everything within myself that is blocking this love right now.

As I find peace within myself, help me to extend it outward and become an instrument of peace to the world.

I adore you and thank you so much.

Amen.

Prayer to Raise the Vibration of the World

*Dearest God, please allow all of us to rise to a higher level
of consciousness where peace prevails on Earth.*

Help us release all negative and fearful energy now.

Allow us to see your love within each person.

*Take away anything that blinds us from
experiencing this total love.*

Please release negativity from all world leaders.

*Allow them to see that love and forgiveness are the most
powerful weapons, and allow only leaders who will
maintain peace to remain in a position of power.*

*Allow your love to dispel all darkness from everyone
involved in terroristic activities.*

*Let this love permeate them now so that they will never
want to harm anyone again.*

*Let your love shine through in the media so that love
and peace are the main focus, not war and violence.*

*Allow those in the media to understand that they bring
more energy to what they cover, so allow them to
deliberately cover more peaceful, positive events
that are happening in this world.*

*We thank you, God, and all your wonderful angels for
allowing us to experience only peace from this point on.*

*We are sorry for the error of our ways in the past,
but that is all behind us now.*

At this time and forevermore, may peace prevail on Earth.

And so it is.

Prayer to Become an Instrument of Peace

*God, please show me what I can do to become
an instrument of your peace.*

*Guide me to perfect situations each and every day where
I may be of service to my fellow man.*

*Assist me in putting my ego aside so I may fully be able
to perceive the needs of others.*

*In coming to the aid of my fellow humans, I am helping you,
God, and I'm helping myself as well.*

*Allow me to give as freely to others as you have
given freely to me.*

Help me to respond to every situation with your Divine love.

*Thank you so much for granting me your perfect knowledge
and strength, so that I may always know what I need to
do to maintain peace on Earth.*

Amen.

Peace Prayer to Those in the Celestial Realm

*God, grant me the confidence and ability to become a
true instrument of your peace.*

*I call upon my guardian angels, the archangels, ascended
masters, saints, enlightened beings from other areas of
the universe, and my deceased loved ones to join forces
with me to enhance harmony and raise the
vibration of our beautiful planet.*

*Thank you for clearing out all negativity from our hearts
so that the love that has always existed within us is
able to shine through brightly again.*

*Please continue to recruit, bless, protect, and support
all peacemakers who are willing and able to uplift
our magnificent world.*

Thank you so much for spreading your
Divine love onto all of us.

With your help in this important cause,
peace on Earth will finally become a reality.

And so it is.

Prayer of Peace for Those Who Are Grieving

God, thank you for all you have given me, especially for
placing [names of deceased loved ones] in my life.

Although they are no longer here in their physical bodies,
I know they are with you and are very much at peace.

Allow me to feel your presence and their presence as well.

Thank you so much for watching over them and for
guiding and protecting me too.

Grant that I can move on peacefully in my life with
the wonderful knowledge that they truly are okay.

I am so grateful that you are always with me and
are helping me every step of the way.

I love you so much.

Prayer for All Living Creatures and the Environment

Dearest God,

Help us to show compassion for all sentient beings,
and enable us to see through their eyes.

Open up our hearts and increase our understanding
of what we can do to save them from harm.

Steer us away from interfering with them in their natural
habitat unless they are in need of our help.

*Remind us to eat with compassion and recognize the
wonderful alternatives we all have that don't include
slaughtering, neglecting, or disregarding their precious lives.*

*Grant that we become more aware of animal-friendly
clothing, products, and hobbies.*

*Show us the steps we can take to protect and support our
magnificent planet that you have entrusted to our care.*

*Enable us to see that we truly can make a difference and
uplift the Earth back to its true state of perfection.*

*Grant that we take our responsibilities as caretakers
of our world seriously, from this day forward.*

Amen.

Prayer for the Environment

*Enable me to fully recognize how my actions
are affecting this beautiful world.*

*Show me the steps I can take to heal the Earth,
and guide me how to educate others to do the same.*

*Instill this important wisdom within all the
decision-makers of industries and those in public office.*

*Enable them to understand the urgency of this message
and the consequences of putting profits ahead
of the well-being of the environment.*

*Grant all of us the strength to take on this
essential task of protecting our only home.*

*From this day forward, may we comprehend that
the future of our beloved planet is truly in our hands.*

And so it is.

A Prayer for Animals
attributed to Albert Schweitzer

Hear our humble prayer, O God, for our friends
the animals, especially for animals that are suffering;

for animals that are overworked, underfed, and cruelly treated;

for all wistful creatures in captivity that beat
their wings against bars;

for any that are hunted or lost or deserted
or frightened or hungry;

for all that must be put to death. We entreat for them all thy
mercy and pity, and for those who deal with them we ask a
heart of compassion and gentle hands and kind words.

Make us, ourselves, to be true friends to animals,
and so to share the blessings of the merciful.

Prayer of Saint Francis

Lord, make me an instrument of thy peace.

Where there is hatred, let me sow love;

Where there is injury, pardon;

Where there is doubt, faith;

Where there is despair, hope;

Where there is darkness, light;

Where there is sadness, joy.

O divine Master, grant that I may not so much seek
To be consoled as to console,

To be understood as to understand,

To be loved as to love;

For it is in giving that we receive;

It is in pardoning that we are pardoned;

It is in dying to self that we are born to eternal life.

Peace Prayers from All Major Religions

These prayers for peace were offered in Assisi, Italy, on the Day of Prayer for World Peace during the UN International Year of Peace, 1986.

A Baha'i Prayer for Peace

Be generous in prosperity and thankful in adversity.

Be fair in thy judgment and guarded in thy speech.

*Be a lamp unto those who walk in darkness
and a home to the stranger.*

*Be eyes to the blind and a guiding light
unto the feet of the erring.*

*Be a breath of life to the body of humankind,
a dew to the soil of the human heart,
and a fruit upon the tree of humility.*

A Buddhist Prayer for Peace

*May all beings everywhere plagued with sufferings of
body and mind quickly be freed from their illnesses.*

*May those frightened cease to be afraid,
and may those bound be free.*

*May the powerless find power and may people
think of befriending one another.*

*May those who find themselves in trackless, fearful
wildernesses—the children, the aged, the unprotected—
be guarded by beneficent celestials, and may they
swiftly attain Buddhahood.*

A Christian Prayer for Peace

*Blessed are the peacemakers, for they shall be
called the children of God.* (Matthew 5:9)

*But I say to you that hear, love your enemies;
do good to those who hate you; bless those who curse you;
pray for those who abuse you. To those who strike you on
the cheek, offer the other also; and from those who take
away your cloak, do not withhold your coat as well.*

*Give to everyone who begs from you, and
of those who take away your goods, do not ask
them again. And as you wish that others would
do to you, do so to them.* (Luke 6:27–31)

A Hindu Prayer for Peace

Oh God, lead us from the unreal to the Real.

Oh God, lead us from darkness to light.

Oh God, lead us from death to immortality.

Shanti, Shanti, Shanti unto all.

*Oh Lord God almighty, may there be
peace in celestial regions.*

May there be peace on Earth.

May the waters be appeasing.

*May herbs be wholesome, and may trees
and plants bring peace to all.*

May all beneficent beings bring peace to us.

May the Vedic Law propagate peace all through the world.

May all things be a source of peace to us.

*And may thy peace itself bestow peace on all
and may that peace come to me also.*

An Islamic Prayer for Peace

In the Name of Allah, the beneficent, the merciful:

Praise be to the Lord of the Universe who has created us and made us into tribes and nations that we may know each other, not that we may despise each other.

If the enemy incline toward peace, do thou also incline toward peace, and trust in God, for the Lord is one that hears and knows all things.

And the servants of God Most Gracious are those who walk on the Earth in humility, and when we address them, we say, "Peace."

A Jain Prayer for Peace

Peace and Universal Love is the essence of the Gospel preached by all the Enlightened Ones.

The Lord has preached that equanimity is the Dharma.

I forgive all creatures, and may all creatures forgive me.

Unto all have I amity, and unto none, enmity.

Know that violence is the root cause of all miseries in the world.

Violence in fact is the knot of bondage. "Do not injure any living being." This is the eternal, perennial, and unalterable way of spiritual life.

A weapon, however powerful it may be, can always be superseded by a superior one; but no weapon can be superior to nonviolence and love.

A Jewish Prayer for Peace

Come, let us go to the mountain of the Lord,
that we may walk the paths of the Most High.

And we shall beat our swords into ploughshares
and our spears into pruning hooks.

Nation shall not lift up sword against nation;
neither shall they learn war any more.

And none shall be afraid, for the mouth
of the Lord of Hosts has spoken.

A Native African Prayer for Peace

Almighty God, the Great Thumb we cannot
evade to tie any knot,

the Roaring Thunder that splits mighty trees,

the all-seeing Lord on high who sees even the footprints
of an antelope on a rock mass here on Earth,

you are the one who does not hesitate to respond to our call.

You are the cornerstone of peace.

A Native American Prayer for Peace

O Great Spirit of our Ancestors, we raise the pipe to you,
to your messengers the four winds, and to
Mother Earth who provides for your children.

Give us the wisdom to teach our children to love,
to respect, to be kind to each other so that they
may grow with peace in mind.

Let us learn to share all the good things that you
provide for us on this Earth.

A Shinto Prayer for Peace

Although the people living across the ocean surrounding us,
I believe, are all our brothers and sisters, why are
there constant troubles in this world?

Why do winds and waves rise in the ocean surrounding us?

I only earnestly wish that the wind will soon puff away all
the clouds which are hanging over the tops of the mountains.

A Sikh Prayer for Peace

God judges us according to our deeds,
not the coat that we wear.

Truth is above everything, but higher still is truthful living.

Know that we attain God when we love, and only
that victory endures in consequence
of which no one is defeated.

A Zoroastrian Prayer for Peace

We pray to God to eradicate all the misery in the world, that
understanding triumph over ignorance, that generosity triumph
over contempt, and that truth triumph over falsehood.

APPENDIX D

Quotes about Peace

I have found great comfort and inspiration with the following quotes. I suggest that you read through the list, then pick one each day to contemplate in meditation.

"Peace cannot be kept by force; it can only be achieved by understanding."
— Albert Einstein

"Peace is a daily, a weekly, a monthly process, gradually changing opinions, slowly eroding old barriers, quietly building new structures."
— John F. Kennedy

"A mind at peace, a mind centered and not focused on harming others, is stronger than any physical force in the universe."
— Dr. Wayne W. Dyer

"Darkness cannot drive out darkness; only light can do that. Hate cannot drive out hate; only love can do that."
— Martin Luther King, Jr.

"It's rather easy to shine in the light, but to glow in the dark—that's mastery!"
— Rick Beneteau

"If the human race wishes to have a prolonged and indefinite period of material prosperity, they have only got to behave in a peaceful and helpful way toward one another."
— Winston Churchill

"There is a higher court than courts of justice, and that is the court of conscience. It supersedes all other courts."
— Mahatma Gandhi

"Never doubt that a small group of thoughtful, committed citizens can change the world. Indeed, it is the only thing that ever has."
— Margaret Mead

"We look forward to the time when the Power of Love will replace the Love of Power. Then will our world know the blessings of Peace."
— Attributed to William Ewart Gladstone

"There is one question that no one will ask of those who use violence to make their point: What hurts you so bad that you feel you have to hurt me in order to heal it? This does not condone violence, but it can help us to understand it—and to understand how to stop it. [The book *Conversations with God*] says, 'No one does anything inappropriate, given their model of the world.' Embracing the wisdom in those eleven words could change the course of human history."
— Neale Donald Walsch

"If you want to make peace, you don't talk to your friends. You talk to your enemies."

— Moshe Dayan

"Democracy is necessary to peace and to undermining the forces of terrorism."

— Benazir Bhutto

"If we have no peace, it is because we have forgotten that we belong to each other."

— Mother Teresa

"Peace I leave with you; my peace I give you. I do not give to you as the world gives. Do not let your hearts be troubled and do not be afraid."

— Jesus (John 14:27)

"I offer you peace. I offer you love. I offer you friendship. I see your beauty. I hear your need. I feel your feelings."

— Mahatma Gandhi

"Mankind is not the only animal that laughs, cries, thinks, feels, and loves. The sooner we acknowledge that animals are emotional beings, the sooner we will cease destroying animals and embrace them as our brothers and sisters."

— Anthony Douglas Williams

"We but mirror the world. All the tendencies present in the outer world are to be found in the world of our body. If we could change ourselves, the tendencies in the world would also change. As a man changes his own nature, so does the attitude of the world change towards him."

— Mahatma Gandhi

"If you want to make peace with your enemy, you have to work with your enemy. Then he becomes your partner."

— Nelson Mandela

"Peace does not mean an absence of conflicts; differences will always be there. Peace means solving these differences through peaceful means; through dialogue, education, knowledge; and through humane ways."

— Dalai Lama

"Nonviolence isn't about putting the right person in power; it's about awakening the right kind of power in people."

— Michael Nagler

"If you want others to be happy, practice compassion. If you want to be happy, practice compassion."

— Dalai Lama

"Violence is impractical because it is a descending spiral ending in destruction for all. It is immoral because it seeks to humiliate the opponent rather than win his understanding: it seeks to annihilate rather than convert. Violence is immoral because it thrives on hatred rather than love. It destroys community and makes brotherhood impossible. It leaves society in monologue rather than dialogue. Violence ends up defeating itself. It creates bitterness in the survivors and brutality in the destroyers."

— Martin Luther King, Jr.

"To forgive is the highest, most beautiful form of love. In return, you will receive untold peace and happiness."

— Robert Muller

"What kind of peace do we seek? Not a Pax Americana enforced on the world by American weapons of war. Not the peace of the grave or the security of the slave. I am talking about genuine peace, the kind of peace that makes life on Earth worth living, the kind that enables men and nations to grow and to hope and to build a better life for their children . . . not merely peace in our time but peace for all time."

— John F. Kennedy

"I like to believe that people in the long run are going to do more to promote peace than are governments. Indeed, I think that people want peace so much that one of these days governments had better get out of their way and let them have it."

— Dwight D. Eisenhower

"Imagine what 7 billion humans could accomplish if we all loved and respected each other."

— Anthony Douglas Williams

"No one is born hating another person because of the color of his skin, or his background, or his religion. People must learn to hate, and if they can learn to hate, they can be taught to love, for love comes more naturally to the human heart than its opposite."

— Nelson Mandela

"Conflict cannot survive without your participation."

— Dr. Wayne W. Dyer

"Peace begins with a smile."

— Mother Teresa

"Ultimately, we have just one moral duty: to reclaim large areas of peace in ourselves, more and more peace, and to reflect it toward others. And the more peace there is in us, the more peace there will also be in our troubled world."

— Etty Hillesum

"A few really dedicated people can offset the ill effects of masses of out-of-harmony people, so we who work for peace must not falter. We must continue to pray for peace and to act for peace in whatever way we can, we must continue to speak for peace and to live the way of peace; to inspire others, we must continue to think of peace and to know that peace is possible. What we dwell upon we help to bring into manifestation. One little person, giving all of her time to peace, makes news. Many people, giving some of their time, can make history."

— Peace Pilgrim

"IMAGINE A WORLD
Where governments respect the human rights of all their citizens and settle disputes by the rule of law for the common good.

Where all people have food, shelter and access to medical care, and children are born into and raised by healthy families and communities.

Where literacy and education for all are accomplished facts.

Where economic practices create well-being for all stakeholders, including communities and the environment.

Where beauty, the arts, and media inspire the best in people.

Where the benefits of science and technology enhance all circles of life.

Where tolerance and appreciation of diverse religious beliefs is the rule, spiritual practice is encouraged, and reverence for life fostered.

Where the Earth in all her natural beauty is treasured and its resources utilized sustainably, for this and future generations.

This is a world at PEACE . . . May Peace Prevail on Earth. You Are a Pathway to Peace."

— Pathways to Peace (www.PathwaystoPeace.org)

APPENDIX E

Organizations and Websites for Peace

The following are some organizations devoted to the teachings of the concepts of the We Consciousness. See which ones resonate with you; then, if you feel guided, join them in their quest to save our beautiful planet.

www.fourthfreedom.org The Fourth Freedom Forum encourages discussion, development, and dissemination of ideas that will free humanity from the fear of terrorism and war.

www.mettacenter.org Metta Center for Nonviolence is a charity dedicated to the safe and effective use of nonviolence.

www.worldpeace.org The World Peace Prayer Society is a grass-roots global movement to spread the message of the prayer *May Peace Prevail on Earth.*

www.pathwaystopeace.org Pathways to Peace is an educational and consulting organization dedicated to making peace a practical reality through both local and global projects.

www.forusa.org The Fellowship of Reconciliation is an interfaith organization promoting active nonviolence as a means of radical change.

www.agnt.org Association for Global New Thought is an association of churches and centers within the Unity, Religious Science, and nondenominational New Thought spiritual communities dedicated to spiritually guided activism.

www.onegreenplanet.org One Green Planet is is an online platform focused on sustainable food, animal welfare issues, environmental protection, and cruelty-free/green living.

www.internationaldayofpeace.org The International Day of Peace is observed around the world each year on September 21. Established in 1981 by the UN, Peace Day provides a globally shared date for all humanity to commit to peace above all differences and to contribute to building a Culture of Peace.

www.peace-action.org Peace Action is a national grassroots organization that promotes U.S. foreign policy based on peaceful support for human rights and democracy, eliminating the threat of weapons of mass destruction, and cooperation with the world community.

www.peacealliance.org The Peace Alliance is an alliance of organizers and advocates throughout the U.S. that's taking the work of peace building from the margins of society into the centers of national discourse and policy priorities.

www.healthyselfesteem.org The National Association for Self-Esteem aims to fully integrate self-esteem into the fabric of American society so that every individual experiences personal worth and happiness.

www.mclveganway.org.uk The Movement for Compassionate Living is committed to working nonviolently for change, promoting lifestyles that are possible for all the world's people, sustainable within the resources of the planet, environmentally friendly, and free of all exploitation of animals and people.

www.vegansociety.com The Vegan Society is a nonprofit that promotes veganism as an easily adopted and widely recognized approach to reducing animal and human suffering.

www.vegan.org Vegan Action works to eliminate animal suffering, reduce environmental impacts, and improve human health through the promotion of vegan diets.

www.foei.org Friends of the Earth International is the world's largest grassroots environmental network, uniting 71 diverse national member groups and 5,000 local activist groups on every continent to campaign on today's most urgent environmental and social issues.

ACKNOWLEDGMENTS

To Ken, thank you for always being so patient, kind, helpful, encouraging, and my biggest supporter in all that I do! You are the wind beneath my wings, and I love you. My wish is for you to see through my eyes and recognize the beautiful light that you are. I am so blessed to have you in my life!

To Chris, my firstborn, you now can fully understand the depth of the love a parent can have for his or her children. I've always been so proud of you. You always aim for perfection in all that you do, and now your latest, and perhaps most important achievement, is being such an amazing father to Annabelle and Miles!

To Jessica, I can't believe how quickly the years have gone by. There are no words to describe how wonderful it has been watching you grow up to become the amazing woman that you now are. Your whole being radiates the tremendous love you are experiencing in your life! You are a fantastic mother to Emily, giving her the irreplaceable gift of your time, patience, and tenderheartedness. You are now going to share this special gift with so many other children as you begin your latest journey with JEM Yoga. I'm so proud of you!

To Tim, thanks for really understanding who I am and always encouraging me to think outside the box. You effortlessly demonstrate how to live life to the fullest and cherish each moment of your journey here on

Earth. I love that you continually reach out for newer and deeper experiences and always stand out from the crowd. I will always support you in all you do! You are an inspiration to me.

To Jamie, thank you for your complete compassion for *all* animals and for passing that kindness down to my grandchildren. As a fellow vegan, I fully understand how essential it is to remain strong with these convictions even when most of society is eating animals and living in a different way. As you know, I'm absolutely with you every step of the way! You are an incredible mother, teaching your children perfect manners and respect for all of life.

To Steve, thank you for being a wonderful son-in-law. I've known you for so many years, but have never seen you happier than you are now. You are such an incredible husband to Jessica and father to Emily. Cherish each and every moment, because time flies by, as you are seeing already.

To Annabelle, Emily, and Miles, the next generation of peacemakers. May you always remember the Divine beings that you are and create amazing miracles in your lives! The future of the world is in your precious hands.

To Marcelene, I am so thankful that Wayne brought us together. You are one of the kindest and most peaceful souls I have ever met! You have raised such incredible children—each one so distinct from the others, yet each one equally gorgeous, inside and out!

To Skye, you are beyond sweet! Your beautiful voice and gentleness represent the angel that you are. Remember to be fearless in all you do and always continue to sing. Get ready for wonderful new beginnings! It's all happening now!

To Sommer, you are on such an awesome path right now. Remember, your dad loves you so much, is so proud of you, and is with you every step of the way!

To Serena, your words of encouragement have meant more to me than you will ever know! I *love* your free spirit and outspokenness. As your dad says, you will be the "voice box" that will keep his teachings alive.

To Sands, I'm so glad I finally met you in Maui! Thanks for the breathtaking sailing experience on the Gemini. I know that your dad is so pleased that you are finally living your dream!

To Saje, you are the one who brought us all together! Without you, none of this would have occurred. It has been such a wonderful experience working together with you on our workshops about life after death. Also, thank you for being such an amazing babysitter for my granddaughter, Emily. My daughter and Emily adore you—and so do I!

To Tracy, I love our late-night discussions about significant world events. When you talk, I feel that your dad is speaking directly through you! Thank you for being my dance partner at Saje's wedding!

To those at Hay House who have worked with me on this important project—especially my editor, Nicolette Salamanca Young. You are the best!

To Reid Tracy, thank you for believing in this message and for allowing Wayne's voice to be heard again.

To Brett Bevell, thank you for giving me the incredible opportunity to stay at the Hermitage in Omega to write this book. It was truly a life-changing experience!

To all those who share my dream of a peaceful world, I'm passing my torch to you!

To Saint Francis of Assisi and the rest of the We Guides, thank you for choosing me to become your instrument of peace at this critical time on Earth.

To Wayne Dyer, I salute you! Thank you for all you've done for humankind when you were here in the physical and for continuing to spread your amazing message of hope from where you are now!

ABOUT THE AUTHOR

Karen Noé is a renowned New Jersey–based psychic medium, spiritual counselor, and healer with a two-year waiting list. She is the author of *Your Life After Their Death: A Medium's Guide to Healing After a Loss* and *Through the Eyes of Another: A Medium's Guide to Creating Heaven on Earth by Encountering Your Life Review Now.* She is the founder of the Angel Quest Center in New Jersey, where she teaches classes, gives readings, and practices alternative healing.

After best-selling author Dr. Wayne W. Dyer left the physical plane in 2015, Karen has consistently been receiving very profound and specific messages from him for his family and for the world as well. While Wayne comes through to Karen singularly, he also comes through together with a group of other celestial beings called the We Guides, which includes Saint Francis of Assisi and countless other angels and ascended masters.

To sign up for Karen's newsletter and to find out more about her, please visit her website at www.karennoe.com.

Hay House Titles of Related Interest

YOU CAN HEAL YOUR LIFE, the movie,
starring Louise Hay & Friends
(available as a 1-DVD program, an expanded
2-DVD set, and an online streaming video)
Learn more at www.hayhouse.com/louise-movie

THE SHIFT, the movie,
starring Dr. Wayne W. Dyer
(available as a 1-DVD program, an expanded
2-DVD set, and an online streaming video)
Learn more at www.hayhouse.com/the-shift-movie

*BRIDGING TWO REALMS: Learn to Communicate
with Your Loved Ones on the Other-Side,* by John Holland

*EATERNITY: More than 150 Deliciously Easy Vegan Recipes
for a Long, Healthy, Satisfied, Joyful Life!,* by Jason Wrobel

*FROM DEEP SPACE WITH LOVE: A Conversation about
Consciousness, the Universe, and Building a Better World,*
by Mike Dooley with Tracy Farquhar

*IF YOU COULD TALK TO AN ANGEL: Angelic Answers to
Your Questions on Life, Love, Purpose, and More,* by Gerry Gavin

*VISIONS, TRIPS, AND CROWDED ROOMS:
Who and What You See Before You Die,* by David Kessler

All of the above are available at your local bookstore,
or may be ordered by contacting Hay House (see next page).

We hope you enjoyed this Hay House book. If you'd like to receive our online catalog featuring additional information on Hay House books and products, or if you'd like to find out more about the Hay Foundation, please contact:

Hay House, Inc., P.O. Box 5100, Carlsbad, CA 92018-5100
(760) 431-7695 or (800) 654-5126
(760) 431-6948 (fax) or (800) 650-5115 (fax)
www.hayhouse.com® • www.hayfoundation.org

———

Published in Australia by: Hay House Australia Pty. Ltd.,
18/36 Ralph St., Alexandria NSW 2015
Phone: 612-9669-4299 • *Fax:* 612-9669-4144
www.hayhouse.com.au

Published in the United Kingdom by: Hay House UK, Ltd.,
The Sixth Floor, Watson House, 54 Baker Street, London W1U 7BU
Phone: +44 (0)20 3927 7290 • *Fax:* +44 (0)20 3927 7291
www.hayhouse.co.uk

Published in India by: Hay House Publishers India,
Muskaan Complex, Plot No. 3, B-2, Vasant Kunj, New Delhi 110 070
Phone: 91-11-4176-1620 • *Fax:* 91-11-4176-1630
www.hayhouse.co.in

———

Access New Knowledge.
Anytime. Anywhere.

Learn and evolve at your own pace
with the world's leading experts.

www.hayhouseU.com

Listen. Learn. Transform.

Reach your fullest potential with unlimited Hay House audios!

Gain access to endless wisdom, inspiration, and encouragement from world-renowned authors and teachers—guiding and uplifting you as you go about your day. With the *Hay House Unlimited* Audio app, you can learn and grow in a way that fits your lifestyle . . . and your daily schedule.

With your membership, you can:

- Let go of old patterns, step into your purpose, live a more balanced life, and feel excited again.

- Explore thousands of audiobooks, meditations, immersive learning programs, podcasts, and more.

- Access exclusive audios you won't find anywhere else.

- Experience completely unlimited listening. No credits. No limits. No kidding.

Try for FREE!

Hay House Podcasts
Bring Fresh, Free Inspiration Each Week!

Hay House proudly offers a selection of life-changing audio content via our most popular podcasts!

Hay House Meditations Podcast

Features your favorite Hay House authors guiding you through meditations designed to help you relax and rejuvenate. Take their words into your soul and cruise through the week!

Dr. Wayne W. Dyer Podcast

Discover the timeless wisdom of Dr. Wayne W. Dyer, world-renowned spiritual teacher and affectionately known as "the father of motivation." Each week brings some of the best selections from the 10-year span of Dr. Dyer's talk show on Hay House Radio.

Hay House Podcast

Enjoy a selection of insightful and inspiring lectures from Hay House Live events, listen to some of the best moments from previous Hay House Radio episodes, and tune in for exclusive interviews and behind-the-scenes audio segments featuring leading experts in the fields of alternative health, self-development, intuitive medicine, success, and more! Get motivated to live your best life possible by subscribing to the free Hay House Podcast.

Find Hay House podcasts on iTunes, or visit www.HayHouse.com/podcasts for more info.